Making the Big Leap

coach yourself to create the life you really want

SUZY GREAVES

NEW HOLLAND PUBLISHERS

To Jools and Charlie, the two loves of my life.

First published in 2004 by New Holland Publishers (UK) Ltd
London • Cape Town • Sydney • Auckland

www.newhollandpublishers.com

Garfield House, 86–88 Edgware Road, London, W2 2EA, United Kingdom

80 McKenzie Street, Cape Town 8001, South Africa

14 Aquatic Drive, Frenchs Forest, NSW 2086, Australia

218 Lake Road, Northcote, Auckland, New Zealand

ISBN 1 84330 742 1

Publishing Manager: Jo Hemmings
Editors: Deborah Taylor and Charlotte Judet
Designer: Nicky Barneby
Jacket Designer: Ian Hughes
Production Controller: Joan Woodroffe

Author photograph by Andrew Montgomery

Reproduction by Modern Age Repro company, Hong Kong
Printed and bound by Kyodo Printing Co (Singapore) Pte Ltd

Read this book if:

- You get on the treadmill every morning and think 'there has to be another way.'
- You've just had your own personal wake up call and you're committed to finding another way to live your life.
- You find yourself thinking regularly 'I just can't do this any longer.'
- You don't want to struggle through life – you want to find a life that delights you.
- You are prepared to think differently, not just do something different.
- You are prepared to be the creator of your life, not the victim of it.
- You want a life that you adore.

Contents

Introduction

'I can't do this anymore.'

Seven years ago, I woke up.

I woke up 30 miles from home at the end of the tube line, having slept through my stop, and thought – 'I can't do this anymore.' I was a journalist and worked 16 hours a day, six days a week, grind, grind, non-stop. I was tired. All the time. My whole day was spent fighting a bone-crushing fatigue that seemed to eat me up from the inside out until all I could do was cushion myself on the sofa every night lest the slightest knock shattered me into tiny, brittle pieces.

Waking up with two other snoring strangers at the end of a tube line in the wilds of Essex, I felt like I'd found the elephant's graveyard. Except it was where the commuters went to die. And it certainly looked like we were dying – grey faced, our deep-sleep creases looking like battle scars.

How had life turned into this great war? And more to the point – why was I losing it? From the outside, it didn't look like I was losing it. In fact, life looked great. I was married to a man I loved, I had the job of my dreams writing for glossy magazines, and I lived in an apartment in a trendy part of London. I had everything I said I wanted – so why was life this hard? Why was I so damn tired all the time? Why did I feel this gnawing discontent that had me crawling into a bottle of wine every night to make me feel better? Coffee to get me going, cigarettes to keep me going and a bottle of wine to make me stop.

I wasn't alone. Everywhere I looked, there were the same grim faces, the same scars whether they were those of my friends and colleagues at work, my friends who stayed at home looking after the children, or my fellow combatants on the tube. It was the same look, the same mantra: 'I'm so stressed, I'm so tired.' It was more worrying when it all went quiet, when we slipped into that quiet resignation, that inertia, the joyless acceptance of: 'Well, that's just how it is, just get on with it.'

I woke up on the tube that evening and knew that if I accepted that this is just how life is, I'd be on that train for the rest of my life, constantly fighting to stay out of the commuter's graveyard. And I didn't want to struggle any more. That evening, I woke up and thought 'NO'. I wanted to shake my fellow commuters awake and scream: 'It doesn't have to be this way. It doesn't, it doesn't, it doesn't.'

But I wasn't really screaming at them, I was screaming at myself. And it was the silent scream that woke me up. I realized that I wanted a life that delighted me – and that I had to go and get it.

I woke up and hired a coach; a Life Coach. I know it sounds too self-indulgent for words and being a 'call a spade a shovel' Northerner, I had similar prejudices. But who better to help me on my quest for a better life?

Seven years ago, I told my coach: 'I can't do this anymore.' She didn't ask what the 'this' was but asked what I wanted instead. 'I want a life I adore', I said. 'A life with plenty of time, money, space, lots of lovely friends and a job you'd pay to do. I want to bubble over again. I want to sing in the shower. I want my bounce back.'

What I wanted was a life full of holidays in the Caribbean, earning three times more than I did, being nuzzled non-stop by my husband and never having to screen telephone calls to avoid speaking to so-called friends who vampired every ounce of energy that I had left after a gruelling day. And no more gruelling days – just some kind of work that would make every day feel like a holiday. I didn't want to feel tired, fed up and as if I was dragging myself around life. I wanted to feel content, peaceful and to feel that I was 'in' my life rather than on the outside desperately looking through a window begging to be let in.

I got excited for a second before reality elbowed me firmly in the ribs. Contented? Peaceful? Earn three times my salary? I couldn't afford a holiday to Cardiff never mind the Caribbean. My husband was more into guzzling beer than nuzzling me. Every day like a holiday? Who was I kidding? Then came the question that changed my life:

What would you have to believe about yourself for this dream to come true?

I blustered, I sneered, I sneered a bit more, but in the end I wept. I realized that for me to get a life I adored, the thing that was going to have to change was me. I didn't believe in me. I didn't believe I was good enough, clever enough, beautiful enough, witty enough, *anything* enough to manifest even a tiny piece of my dream life.

That question was my gateway into this other life where I got my bounce back. It made me realize that if I wanted to transform my external world, I'd have to change my internal one. Through my own journey, and now from coaching hundreds of my own clients, I have discovered that if you don't believe you're good enough and if you listen to the voice of fear which beats you up regularly, what happens is that you can't say no; you put up with stuff you don't want to put up with and you work all day and night to prove that you are worthy of a place in the world. And now of course, I'm a convert. In fact, I was so impressed, I bought the company, as it were. I have since trained to become a coach myself and set up my own coaching company.

This book is for those who've also heard that same cry for more. Yours might not be a scream but merely a whisper – that little voice inside your head that nudges you every time you book a holiday, read another self-help book, buy a lottery ticket or climb into that fabulous bottle of wine that promises escape – the whisper that says: 'There has to be another way, there has to be another way, there has to be another way.'

This book is about finding that other way. It's about finding a way to live a life that inspires, fulfills and delights you. Over and over again I see my clients, doing as I did, pleasing others rather than themselves, spending time with people they don't even like, and working like dogs just to buy clothes, cars and houses to prove to themselves and to others that they're somebody. It's not surprising they feel like crap if they spend their lives in an exhausting pantomime that actually has nothing to do with what they want but everything to do with their fears of who they think they're not.

Finding another way doesn't necessarily mean you'll be changing career, moving to France and buying a vineyard, downsizing or downshifting, getting a divorce or anything as radical as that. As I discovered on my journey – and in that very first coaching session – the 'Big Leap' doesn't necessarily involve changing what we do (or what we buy), it's more about changing how we think and feel about ourselves. It's not particularly about DOING something different, it's about THINKING something different.

However, I have naturally attracted clients who also want to make a 'Big Leap' in the external world too. Probably because in my own life I have made the internal Big Leap but also the external one – I'm building a life on my terms, living it how I want to live it – working from home, building a business around my own personal passion.

Making the Big Leap is not just about changing your career, it's about shaking up your whole life and finding a new way of working, living and being. Maybe you don't want to commute any more, or perhaps you simply don't want to work for a company or boss who doesn't value you. Maybe you want to work for yourself and create a thriving business or have a freelance career being paid for who you are not just for what you do. Or maybe you want to live a radically different life.

My clients have wanted many things: to leave the corporate world behind to write books, to live by the beach and have sand between their toes, or to create global brands based on their personal passion for handbags; but most of all, they all wanted to be happy, fulfilled and passionate about their work and their life.

I believe Big Leapers are pioneers who are part of a new ground-swell of voices shouting: 'No, enough! We don't have to live this way, we don't have to sell our souls, sell our dreams, commute three hours a day, never see our kids, our loved ones and slowly watch our lives whimper away.' Big Leapers are holding up a light, laughing and leading the way, saying: 'Don't compromise, there is another way, let's do it our way, let's create it the way we want, let's live a fabulous life.'

Making the Big Leap is a handbook for the Big Leap generation. It's a guide to help you on your journey. We have left the 20th century behind and with it, the rules that told us how to sit, behave and live our lives. We now have the freedom to choose a life and create it any way we want. But that freedom comes with a price because as we are no longer told what we 'should' be doing, we are left with uncertainty so we question ourselves constantly about our choices – 'Am I doing this right? Is my way wrong? Am I simply fooling myself?'

This book will hopefully keep you sane and will hold your hand along the way. What it offers is not so much a 'how to' process, but rather a guide that shines the light of awareness on your fears and blocks so that you will be better equipped to steer a path around them.

The Five Step Big Leap journey

I have created a five-step model so that you will have the right signposts to follow on the Big Leap journey. In Step 1 I will be challenging you to come out of denial and to start identifying what it is that you don't want in your life any more. In Step 2 of the journey, I will help you to identify what it is that you do want. In Step 3 the Big Leap begins in earnest as I ask you to stretch yourself by exploring your belief systems. By Step 4 you will be really going for the Big Leap, as you find out your little scams that keep you stuck in your old life. In Step 5 you'll tackle your saboteurs and make the all-important commitment to action as you truly change your life.

Five Steps to the Big Leap

1 You will identify what you don't want in your life anymore.
2 You will identify how you want your life to be.
3 You will explore your belief systems and find out what's holding you back.
4 You will discover your little scams – the behaviours and actions that keep you stuck.
5 Finally, you'll tackle your saboteurs and commit to taking action to build your dream life.

The Big Leap Cheerleaders

Because the Big Leap journey can be lonely at times, I've invited some guests along. I have asked seven of my clients who have made or who are in the process of making the Big Leap, to contribute to the book by giving their advice, practical tips and words of wisdom to help you along the way.

Meet your Big Leap support team:

Nicky Hambleton Jones, 32, came to coaching in January 2001. She was a management consultant but was made redundant in the first week of our coaching together. It was the third time this had happened to Nicky. She never wanted to be in this position ever again and wanted to create her own business and brand around something she was passionate about. Nicky had a passion for fashion and I coached her around starting her own fashion-styling business Tramp2Vamp! (see Useful Web Addresses on page 169 for more information). Nicky created her own business, website and brand and now has her own make-up range, which is available through her website. In 2003, she was signed up by Channel 4 in the UK to present her own TV show, 10 Years Younger, on helping people to shed years from their appearance.

Lynne McNicoll, 47, had not worked for eight years when first hired me as her coach in September 2002. Primarily she sought coaching because she wanted to find new motivation to lose weight. Lynne was a housewife living in Edinburgh when we started working together, but six months later she had made the Big Leap and created her own business working from home as a 'virtual assistant', a PA who works for many clients from home, handling their needs through email and the Internet.

Rachel Dobson, 30, came to coaching in May 2003. She was senior features writer at a national Sunday tabloid, but wanted to leave the 9 to 5 lifestyle behind and create a freelance life and business. She resigned in August 2003 and is currently a freelance features journalist and is setting up her own business as a property developer.

Salma Shah, 35, works as an account manager in IT sales and came to coaching in September 2003. She has trained as a coach and is currently setting up her own life coaching company, The Lifeskills Company (see Useful Web Addresses on page 169 for more information). She also wants to write for national magazines and newspapers on coaching and self-development.

Donal Doherty, 28, was a bar manager in the City of London when he came to coaching in September 2002. He is now Director of Egoscue Method Clinic in London. Egoscue is a revolutionary method for achieving a pain-free state of optimal health and fitness through correct postural alignment (see Useful Web Addresses on page 169 for more information). Donal is responsible for setting up the first Egoscue Method Clinic in Europe.

Andrew Stone, 32, worked as a journalist on a trade magazine in London. In September 2000, he made the Big Leap and resigned from his job then travelled to Hong Kong to find writing work there. Andrew is now a travel writer for Lonely Planet travel guides and travels everywhere from Ireland to South Africa to Australia to research and write guidebooks..

Christopher Gibbs, 34, worked as an accountant for 13 years. He didn't enjoy his job and it finally began to affect his health to the extent that eventually he was signed off sick with depression in March 2000. He came to coaching in June 2002. He is currently a student of psychology and media at Buckingham University.

I wish I could tell you that making the Big Leap is a five-step quick-fix programme – after all, it might sell this book faster! But if I did, I'd be lying. It takes time to shift your internal landscape so your external scenery can start to look different. I know we're all searching for the magic pill or the silver bullet that will transform our life overnight but this book is not going to give you any false promises. It's an honest book. The Big Leap support team will not pull any punches. They're not going to dress it up for you and tell you it's quick and easy – because sometimes it's not, and it's okay that it's not.

Making the Big Leap requires courage, determination and the ability to laugh at yourself – a lot. The exercises in this book can be life-changing, without a doubt, but the journey is not a fluffy when-I-woke-up-my-life-was-different kind of trip. If only... On this journey, you'll be confronting yourself and coming up against questions that you've probably been avoiding for years. To make the Big Leap you'll probably have to step way out of your comfort zone and be prepared to feel out of your depth, grumpy and downright terrified at times. But it's in that moment of fear that the magic happens, this is where you make the Big Leap and life comes out to catch you. Not once but every time.

Keeping a Big Leap journal

- To get the most out of your journey, I am asking you to create a Big Leap journal.
- Buy a special notebook in which you can write down your answers to the many questions and exercises in this book. You'll find it will be helpful for you to have all your 'answers' in the same place rather than on the backs of envelopes or scraps of paper scattered around the house. It's also great to look back on, to see how far you've come and also to see patterns that emerge.
- I still find it highly encouraging to look back at my own Big Leap journal – the journey of despair from waking up hung-over on a tube train in the wilds of Essex to retraining for a career that inspires me every day and which fills me with so much energy it feels like my hair stands on end.

Let's begin . . .

'Once upon a time. . .'

At this point in the Big Leap process, just before you start making your five-step journey, I need you to sign up and make a commitment – a commitment to suspending belief of what you know of the world so far, a commitment to preparing yourself to enter a world where anything is possible. I need you to commit to doing a 'Harry'.

As in Harry Potter. For I have a theory. The reason why the Harry Potter books have taken the world by storm is that each and every one of us has a little piece of Harry inside of us. We're all wizards at heart. Our hidden power is the ability to change our thoughts.

But somewhere, somehow, we have locked ourselves in the cupboard under the stairs and forgotten who we are – we have forgotten how powerful we are, we have forgotten how to fly and forgotten how to use our wands to create the life we want. Instead of using magic, we choose to live in the Muggle world, where struggle, competition and keeping up with the Dursleys is a full-time occupation. We know this is 'reality' but somehow, we feel out of sorts, we don't seem to fit in the wizard inside feels frustrated and deadened by a life of the Dursleys of 4, Privet Drive with their neat suburban boundaries.

To make the Big Leap you need to wake up: wake up to who you are. And just like Harry receiving his invitation from Hogwarts, I want you to see this book as an invitation to a new magical world. But to get the most out of that world, to get through the platform barrier on platform number 9¾ at Kings Cross Station, to be able to board the Hogwarts Express, you need to believe that another world exists. At this point in the Big Leap journey, you're probably a little bit dubious, so all I need you to do right now is commit to being open to finding this 'other' world, this other way of being.

When I woke up seven years ago, I decided that I couldn't live in the 'Muggle' world any more – whatever I had to do, wherever I had to go, I was not going to live my life like this any more. I was going to find another way. I was going to think differently, I was going to 'do' differently; but I didn't have a clue what that meant. At that point, I simply had to commit to the idea that I would find another way, even if I didn't really know the route.

Unfortunately, sometimes it has to get really bad before we decide we've had enough of the 'Muggle' way of doing things. Sometimes it takes a life-threatening illness, the death of a loved one or simply a misery that seems to seep into our very soul, for us to make the decision to live another way.

Maybe you've picked up this book because things haven't got that bad yet but they're simply jogging along, day after day and you've thought 'there has to be more to life than this'. Or perhaps you've got the shiny red Ferrari, the house in the country and the career that allows you to go on three holidays a year but you feel that all you've got is the lifestyle without the life. Maybe you just know this can't be all there is. Or perhaps you're heading the other way, and life is about as bad as it can possibly get and you've been living under the proverbial staircase for several years now.

Whether it's just a vague discontent or the horror of discovering you've got breast cancer – whether it's the whisper or the roar you've heard – I'm assuming you're in the process of searching for some answers, for some solutions – or you wouldn't have bought this book. Which is great, but before you start the book, I am asking you to make a commitment to find another way to think, to live, to be – which means a commitment to be open to thinking differently, to thinking 'magically'.

As Harry signed up for Hogwarts' Wizard School, I want you to sign up to learning a different way of doing things, of entering another world where magic can happen, where you leave the 'Muggle world' behind and suspend everything you've believed about life so far so you can re-create it any way you want.

Okay, before you decide to close this book because you think that I'm trying to get you to join a cult, wear a pointed hat and run naked round the garden, let me spell it out for you:

Ten ways to know you're willing to live and think magically

- You don't know 'how' life is going to change, you just know it will.
- You feel very, very excited.
- You feel very, very scared.
- You are willing to reinvent the way you see the world.
- You are willing to reinvent the way you see yourself.
- You are willing to see it when you believe it.
- You know that life is just about to get a whole lot different.
- Deep down you know you have a lot of hidden potential.
- Deep down you know you're very powerful.
- Deep down you believe in magic.

When I woke up on that train seven years ago, I never thought that the life I have now would have been possible. But I knew with every fibre of my being that there was another way. Now I know for sure that none of us needs to live a 'Muggle' life that bores us, exhausts us, or drains every ounce of energy from our soul. We can create the lives we want. We just need to have a re-think and find the courage to get out of our comfort zones so we can find our inner wizard and start thinking magically. The way to start this process is by answering some tough questions, deciding to stop being a victim, and to stop blaming everyone and everything else for what life is offering us. Only then can we start making some different choices. Choices that align us with a different kind of energy – the energy of hope, of hilarity, of happiness. Choices that give us an energy that blows our hair back and makes us remember why we're alive and what our purpose is.

The hardest step is always the first – it means taking responsibility for your life and knowing that only you can change it. It is a big leap and it is momentous and life-altering. And it is also a magical journey.

So, now, if you are ready to take your first step, and if you are ready to make the Big Leap, if you're ready to commit, if you're ready to rewrite your story, I suggest you have your wand at the ready – turn the page and begin.

Big Leap Step 1:
Identify what you don't want

'There has to be more to life than this.'

It is never too late to be what you might have been.
  George Eliot

If you're thinking: 'There has to be more to life than this', then you're at Step 1 of your journey towards making the Big Leap.

On this first step, I will be asking you to really look your life in the eye and be very honest about what is not working for you. It's a challenging process – and it may feel a tad depressing in the middle of this step so be prepared to wonder why you're doing it – but once it's done, you'll know exactly why and you'll certainly be ready to make some changes.

Make sure you don't wallow or stop here too long though. The purpose is to move you out of pain into action, so make sure that when this first step is done, you move on quickly so you can discover how to be who you want to be and do what you want to do.

Big Leap Step 1: Taking the Baby Steps

1 The Boiled Frog syndrome
2 Meet your Inner Pessimist
3 Getting your Needs Met

- 'There has to be more to life than this.'
- 'What am I doing with my life?'
- 'How on earth did I get here?'
- 'I want more!'
- 'I want it all.'
- 'I don't know what I want any more.'

What you're probably doing at Big Leap Step 1

- You go to the bar or pub after work – a lot – or find yourself drinking at home every night.
- You feel envious of other people's lives and bitch about them to all your friends, or anyone who will listen.
- You find yourself obsessively watching TV programmes about how to change your life/garden/house.
- You buy 20 lottery tickets a week.
- You watch more than 10 hours of TV a week.
- You're always busy but never feel as if you're achieving a great deal.
- You feel a vague sense of discontent, even in your happiest moments.

The first step in the Big Leap five-step programme is to come out of denial. This means coming out of the fog and just getting very clear about what you don't want. At this point, you don't have to do anything about it – you just have to tell the truth.

Maybe you have lived in denial for years, numbing yourself with alcohol or recreational drugs or just by watching so much TV that you know the storyline of every soap there is – even the really bad ones!

'How are things?' people ask you. 'You know, okay', you say. You stagger from one weekend to the next, vaguely discontent but not quite being able to put your finger on why. Or maybe you can... Perhaps you blame your misery on your crap boss, or your partner who seems to have lost their sparkle, or those extra pounds of weight that you simply can't shift because deep down, you know that if you admitted what was wrong, you would have to do something about it.

Don't underestimate how much courage it takes to come out of denial and admit your life stinks. It takes a lot.

Like Kate, for instance, who had to admit she hated her career after spending years in training. She was 32 and had spent seven years training to be a doctor but found herself in the bar most nights.

'I just drank and drank. I was desperately unhappy but couldn't admit why. I hated my job but I couldn't admit it to anyone, least of all myself because that meant I'd have to do something about it and that scared me to death.' I asked Kate not to think past this first step. All she had to do was admit the truth about her life as it was now.

'I have just spent my twenties training for a career that gives me prestige and respect in the outside world but I hate every minute, every second of it. I've never wanted to be a doctor. I even hated biology when I was at school. I don't want to be a doctor any more.'

There. It was out – the bare, bald truth of it. Scary stuff, but also liberating for her to say it out loud for the first time.

When we constantly hide the truth about a situation and live in denial – whether it be about our relationship ('I don't love you anymore') or our career ('I can't do this anymore') or our money situation ('I'm £30,000 in debt') – we live with a hole at the bottom our lives: one that drains every ounce of our energy, enthusiasm and passion. No matter how much we eat the right foods or sleep the right amount of hours or drink our eight glasses of water, if we live in denial of what's really not working in our lives, we become so drained of energy that we find ourselves using stimulants or creating dramas or crises to try and jump-start us out of bed every morning.

MAKING THE BIG LEAP:
Nicky Hambleton Jones, 32, Big Leaping from management consultant to celebrity fashion stylist and business owner

When I first came to coaching I was exhausted, trying to fit myself into a lifestyle and job that I hated. I was a management consultant. From the outside, it probably looked like I had a glamorous life – I was always flying overseas to see clients – but I hated it. I felt stupid and worthless and simply didn't fit into the value systems of the company I worked for. I'd find myself working harder and harder, only to feel more insecure. All I'd do was work all the time. I didn't have time to see my friends or even think about finding a boyfriend.

I hired Suzy, my coach, to try and help me work out where I was going wrong. In my first week of coaching I was made redundant. This was the third time this had happened to me. I balled my eyes out. I felt so lost and unhappy. I thought: 'That's it, I've failed, I'm useless.' I had this awful period of a month where I was forced by the redundancy out of denial, I had to admit that I hated my job but had no idea of what to do or where to go next. The thought of starting on the recruitment treadmill filled me with dread. I knew I didn't want to be a consultant any more but I didn't have a clue about what I did what to do.

Looking back, I see that the redundancy was the best thing that could ever have happened to me. It made me come out of denial and stop putting up with a job that I hated. A month later, I had a business idea that filled me with such excitement and enthusiasm, I couldn't imagine doing anything else.

I have learnt that, out of the misery, can come great happiness. It probably took for things to get that bad for me to even consider starting my own business. Pain is a great motivator. So don't worry if you hit that void, when you have no idea where life is going to take you next – or how you're going to pay the bills. That's sometimes exactly the right environment you need to motivate you to take the really big leap that you've been avoiding for years.

Baby Step 1: The Boiled Frog syndrome

Life is not lost by dying; life is lost minute by minute, day by dragging day, in all the thousand small uncaring ways.
Stephen Vincent Benet

I call it the boiled frog syndrome. There is a fact about frogs that isn't particularly pleasant. I don't actually want to know how anyone knows this, but the fact is if you put a frog in water and let the water slowly heat up, the frog will become so soporific that it doesn't jump out but slowly boils to death. However, if you were to put a frog in hot water it would jump out immediately.

It's the same for humans too. Life can get really 'hot' and uncomfortable without us really noticing or acknowledging it. Gradually, it gets worse and worse until our energy is completely drained and we no longer have the stamina to jump out of our situation. Pain is usually our warning system: when we feel pain, we take action to avoid it. But if the 'water' slowly gets hot, we become lulled into a false sense of security. We get used to the heat, we begin to enjoy the heat and then just as it's getting a bit too hot, we become so woozy we can't stir ourselves to action to get out when we need to.

We can all get used to living with a constant feeling of malcontent. How many times have you left behind a difficult situation – by changing jobs, leaving your partner, moving away from a home with the neighbours from hell or simply going on holiday – only to suddenly recognize what you have been tolerating. It's only then that you can look back and wonder: 'How did I ever stand it?'

But we do stand it, and because when we're in it, we think it's normal, we don't feel like we've got a choice. We're stuck in a nightmare but we don't know how to get out of. We feel as if we just have to put up with it. It's a passive state. We're so soporific that if feels like only an act of God or a gargantuan effort could change things – and in the end, to be honest, we just can't be bothered!

Ten ways to tell if you're about to be boiled to death

1 You wake up every morning and switch the snooze button on at least five times.
2 You tell someone about your life/situation and they react in a shocked or horrified way and say things like: 'You don't have to stand for this.'
3 You daydream about your situation coming to an end by way of an act of God – a car accident, a fire, or a tornado (which will whisk you off to the land of Oz, of course).
4 You sleep, watch television, drink or do drugs – a lot.

5 You avoid having conversations about your situation with 'motivated' friends, relatives or colleagues. They don't really understand what it's like and they'll just 'go on' at you.

6 You hang around with other people who are slowly boiling to death, swapping survival skills, saying things like: 'It's warm in here, isn't it?' To which you reply, 'Yeah, but if you keep moving from foot to foot, it's not so bad.'

7 You blame other people – usually one particular person – for what is happening to you and can talk about this person endlessly i.e. how they are impossible to work for/live with etc.

8 You feel you are powerless to change the situation.

9 You drive too fast at inappropriate moments or sleep with inappropriate people or put your life at risk on a weekly basis (see point 3).

10 You are dealing with niggling health problems on a daily basis, like back pain, skin problems, being overweight or becoming increasingly sluggish and lacking in energy.

MAKING THE BIG LEAP:
Christopher Gibbs, 34, Big Leaping from accountancy to becoming a student in media and psychology

Having been in a job for 13 years where things never seemed to get better, I was signed off on sick leave for eight months with severe depression. I knew that I had to change career but didn't know what that other career could be. I knew that I had to change my life to begin enjoying life. What I couldn't understand was why I couldn't enjoy life doing the work that I did.

I refused to go back to a job that made me feel so empty and depressed. It was at this point that I realized I had to bite the bullet and set off in a new direction and find the real me! I wish someone had said to me years ago that I could enjoy work and not slowly sink into the mire of stress and boredom. You don't have to live that way.

I am in the process of making my Big Leap – and finding a new career in the media and arts. No matter how challenging the journey can be at times, it could never be as hideous as seeing my soul seep away day after day in a job I hated. My message to you is – take the Leap – don't wait until you are signed off work with severe depression!

How to get out of the pan without boiling to death

The boiled frog syndrome is probably one of the most dangerous states to be in (it can go on for years) and to make the Big Leap, the first step you have to take is out of the water. So let's turn up the heat so you will leap out.

READY TO LEAP?

EXERCISE: LEAP OUT OF DENIAL

It's not popular to be downbeat. 'Actually my life is crap', would probably not go down well at your Friends Reunited reunion. But in this next exercise, I want you to focus on the simple, unadorned truth. It's time to look yourself in the eye and get brutally honest about your life. It's time to get out the pan of warm water and out of denial. Write it all down. Answer the following questions in your big leap journal.

- What is currently making you unhappy?
- How are you betraying yourself right now?
- How are you playing small in your life?
- What has been the lowest point in the last month? Describe that point in detail. How did it make you feel about yourself?
- What do you have to believe about yourself to create this situation in your life?
- What is the thing you are most afraid to say out loud about your life?
- What are you scared is happening to you?
- If you were run over and killed by a bus tomorrow, what would be your greatest regret?

Okay. Are you depressed yet? If you think that was hard, brace yourself. Because now comes the really tricky bit. I want you to read your answers to a witness. I want you stand up and be counted, to come out of denial and say how you feel about your life – out loud!

A word of warning here. Make sure you choose your witness carefully. Your witness has to be someone who loves you, who is unconditionally supportive. You really don't want to be speaking this out loud to someone who nods and agrees with you or who adds to the list of how rubbish they think you are. Only do this with your best friends and fans. And even with them, coach them to hear your statement supportively. Ask them to simply listen. Tell them that no advice is needed, nor any comments. Your words simply need to be heard in a non-judgmental space. You could perhaps ask them to applaud you after you've finished – if that doesn't feel too touchy-feely – applaud you for your bravery because that's a big step you've just made. The first step is often the hardest and this is a tough one: stating why you're unhappy but not quite knowing where to go next. It's official, you've just stepped out of your comfort zone. Are you feeling sick yet?

MAKING THE BIG LEAP:
Rachel Dobson, 30, Big Leaping from Sunday tabloid journalist to freelance journalist and property developer

The 'leaping out of denial' was my first piece of homework. I was constantly thinking about it, but putting off looking at it. My excuses to myself went from not owning the perfect notebook, to being scared of not finishing and failing.

When eventually I did get down to business, I couldn't stop crying. Bubbling up from the pit of my stomach were big, fat, hot, rolling tears silently dripped off my chin. How the hell did I end up so sad and despairing? I'd set out to do my dream job of being a journalist. I worked with a great team of people and had a good track record, but I abhorred the work I did. I didn't want to write picture captions describing Geri Halliwell's 'fabulous' weight loss when I knew she had an eating disorder. I didn't want to do the 'tits and arse' stories any more.

I felt I only had myself to blame for ending up in such a situation. I thought of my job as an endurance test. But I believed that to earn the money that I earned, you had to put up with this, no questions asked.

The 'lowest point in the month' was the toughest question – how to choose from so many daily occurrences? I remember wishing an injury on myself – a broken leg would have done nicely – just so I could take time off the merry-go-round of work. What must I believe about myself to put up with my work situation day in, day out? When I realized, I thought I must be crackers. I would never expect anyone else to put up with that kind of environment.

At the end, after the tears, I turned on myself, was angry at allowing this to happen to me – after all, nobody else had done this to me.

But that's a good thing in a way. I got myself into this situation and so I could get myself out. You complete an exercise like this and plummet to the depths of despair, but that can be a positive thing because you see that ultimately that you are responsible for your own life. It's just up to us to make the changes. Painful as it may be to see the truth in black and white, it's also incredibly motivating.'

Make a Little Leap

Create a 'Comfort Zone Retreat'. Prepare a list of things to do, people to call, places to go, special foods to eat that you can turn to when life looks bleak and you feel despairing. When I hit rock bottom I usually go to bed, wrap myself in the duvet and demand that my husband feeds me tea and mashed potato. I eat this while watching *Some Like It Hot*. What would our 'Retreat' look like?

Indian meal? Sudds Massage? Bath? Get wine

Victim City!

Rachel makes a good point. When we come out of denial, it's not particularly pleasant and if you're human like the rest of us, it's always good to be able to blame someone else for your misfortunes. Perhaps it's the parents who never gave you the love you needed, the so-called friends who have never supported you, the boss that bullied you, the grandfather who abused you, the wife who spent all your money, the boyfriend who broke your heart, yada, yada, yada . . .

Undoubtedly life can feel very tough at times. But living in Victim City keeps us stuck. It also keeps you safe. After all, here you can blame everyone else for your crap life – your parents, your stressful job, your fascist boss. You can tell yourself it's not your fault. It's out of your control. You can moan and grumble about your life but you don't have to do anything about it. You can keep your macho pride around how stressed and miserable you are intact and remain a martyr to the cause. Poor you!

'Oh, stop being a victim and start getting a life', said my coach in my very first session. Get a life? I didn't even know what that meant. Up until that point, life had happened to me. I had muddled through and I didn't quite realize I had a choice. And there I was in my first session being asked to take responsibility, to be the creator of my life, rather than the victim of it. And it scared the hell out of me.

Because it is scary, you're allowed to say: 'But it's not fair, it's not my fault, they did it to me, I couldn't do anything about it' – but only for 5 minutes. That's all you're allowed. Life can be hard sometimes and it can deal us some tough blows but unless we take responsibility for the part we have played in creating the situation we find ourselves in, we will never be able to find a way out.

Do not misunderstand me. This is NOT about blaming yourself. This is not about beating yourself up about what a stupid/weak/sad person you must have been to have put up with this. This is about becoming self aware enough to recognize certain behaviours or stuff you may have going on that always seems to attract the same kind of heart-breaking men/has you battling with the boss in every job/has you working 16 hours a day when your colleagues work eight.

To make the Big Leap journey, you need to discover for yourself that you don't need to be on a mission to change the world, only on a mission to change yourself or rather your thinking. Whenever you find yourself squirming in your seat and pointing a finger at whoever is ruining your life at that particular moment, take a deep breath then take responsibility for it and put the focus back on to what you can think or do differently to change things.

If I'm honest, I resist doing this as much as the next person. When I'm in a full-scale argument with my husband and I'm enraged by his behaviour, I admit that I don't calmly sit down and think to myself: 'What can I think or do differently here?' I'm too busy jumping up and down and frothing at the mouth. But seven years into my Big Leap journey, I know that I can't get away with making it all about him – at least not for very long. Eventually, I realize that I have to take responsibility – and until I stop frothing and start working out my role in the proceedings, that we'll get nowhere fast.

You may visit Victim City a few times on your Big Leap journey but it's one place that you would be advised to not make your base camp. It might be comfortable but it's full of people, who moan about their lives all the time but never do anything different to change it.

The Misery Interview

Are you ready to make some changes or are you still checked in at Victim City? What do you mean you're still in the water slowly boiling to death? Let's just turn up the heat a tiny bit more, then. Imagine yourself five years from now in the same position you're in today except feeling it five times more intensely. I want you to imagine what your life will be like if you don't change, if you don't come out of denial...

I want you to imagine that a journalist is coming to interview you for a newspaper or magazine for a 'real-life story'. It's the story that editors put on the front of the magazines with headlines like: 'I lost my home, all my money and my husband – in one night!' or: 'I should never have gone under the knife', or: 'I drank myself into poverty'.

Have some fun with the headline of your shock-horror-nightmare story. Imagine the journalist, a rather scruffy one, nail polish slightly chipped and with her roots showing, arriving on your doorstep with her tape recorder at the ready. You have decided to tell your story as a warning to others – about how NOT to do it. This is your Victim City story. Answer the following questions in your journal.

READY TO LEAP?
EXERCISE: CREATE YOUR OWN MISERY INTERVIEW

1   What newspaper or magazine is this for? Is it a down-market local tabloid News of the Losers or a 'rich but lonely' study in a broadsheet? What's the headline?

2   Who reads this newspaper or magazine and why are they fascinated by your story?

3   The interviewer wants to write a description of where you live now

or where the interview is taking place. What does it look like? Is it cardboard city or a large, empty, mansion that you live in all alone?

4   How does the journalist describe you physically? Do you look older than you really are or have the scars of the face lift only just healed? Look at yourself through her eyes.

5   The interviewer asks about your love life. What has happened to you in terms of a relationship or romance that the readers of your article would want to read?

6   The journalist wants a bit of detail about your daily life so describe the worst part of your day, e.g. every morning you get up and realize you are bankrupt and alone.

7   There's a point where the journalist wants you to give the reader a word of warning about how to avoid the pain you've been through. What advice do you want to give people who read this piece?

8   The interviewer asks you to describe the advice you would give to your younger self – what do you say?

9   What's the most interesting part of the article?

10 To make a fitting and dramatic end for the article, the interviewer asks what you think your friends would say about you at your funeral. What do you think would be on your gravestone or written in your obituary? To give you an idea, here's my misery interview:

NEWS OF THE LOSERS Exclusive!
'I threw away my marriage, my health and my life.'

'And no one came, so I just sat there alone in this huge empty room, with a box of cheap wine and slowly drank my way through the lot,' says Suzy Greaves, telling the story of how she celebrated her 40th birthday.

Suzy Greaves lives in a shared house full of students as the house she owned was repossessed when she lost her job, shortly after her husband left her. When she opens the peeling, graffiti-marred door, she is unrecognizable as the successful journalist who interviewed everyone from Richard Harris to Deepak Chopra. The deep lines that travel from her nose to her mouth become cavernous as she sucks on the first of many cigarettes, making her look 20 years older than she actually is.

'I used to have it all – the career, the husband, the house – but inside I was desperately unhappy. I remember waking up on a train in the wilds of Essex, dribbling on a stranger, because I'd slept through my stop. I remember thinking: "There has to be more to life than this." But I didn't know how to change it.'

'I worked all the time, I was just frantic and I never had time for my husband or my friends. And if I did, I just got drunk and then fell asleep. Maybe it was funny in my twenties, but after a while people didn't find it amusing any more. My friends couldn't understand my dysfunctional behaviour – they couldn't understand why I had to work so hard all the time or why I was always getting drunk. But I knew it was the only way I could relax.'

'The harder I worked, the more exhausted I became. I just couldn't be bothered any more. My husband would try and make conversation but I just wanted to slob out after work and I would sit on the same spot on the sofa, watching soap after soap or some crappy TV show and I would just grunt at him. Eventually he stopped making the effort. We became like flat mates and then polite strangers.'

'The saddest thing was that I didn't even notice he'd left me until two days after – when I found the note. I just assumed he was away with his job. I was so drunk when I came in that night that I just didn't see his note pinned to the living room mirror.'

'I have stopped drinking now – since my 40th when my neighbours found me in an alcohol induced coma. I go to an AA meeting every morning. That's how I start the day. Then I tend to watch daytime TV, get something to eat and wait 'til the students get home. I don't really get on with them but at least it breaks up my day. I spend most evenings watching TV. I'm addicted to the soaps. No, I don't go out with my friends. The only friends I had left were heavy drinkers, and I'm worried if I go out with them, I'll fall off the wagon. It's a constant battle not to have a drink. Alcohol tends to dull the pain. Six in the evening is the worst time. That's when I'd usually start drinking. I shake all over and crave the oblivion that alcohol used to give me. The drinking has ruined my fertility too – I can never have children. I always wanted to have a big family. I love children.'

At this point, Greaves walks over to the chipped kitchen counter and puts the kettle on but as she opens the fridge to get out the milk, she pulls out a can of lager. She opens it.

'I like to smell it still', she says before calmly pouring milk in her tea. She brings the can of lager to the table and leaves it open in front of us as she slurps her tea.

'I can't drink any more. I know that it will kill me. My health is pretty much shot to shreds now. My liver is permanently damaged.'

'How did it get to this? I was too scared of change, I suppose. If I could live my life again, I would have woken up on that tube train and done whatever it took to be different. I would have found that "other way". Now I've lost everything. My husband was such a loving man. He's married again now – he's very happy with a beautiful, new wife. "She talks, not slurs", he told me the other day. They're expecting their first child.'

'What would my friends say at my funeral? The sad thing is that probably no one would come. The church would be empty, like the hall at my 40th birthday party.'

At this point Greaves pulls the can of lager to her and takes a big sniff.

Okay, I've been a little over-dramatic but you get the picture. If you look into your future what do you see?

MAKING THE BIG LEAP:

Andrew Stone, 32, Big Leaping from journalist on a trade magazine to travelling the world as a Lonely Planet travel-guide writer

I was 29, living a high old life on The Bookseller, *a London trade magazine. It was a real party magazine – I got the chance to go out to some party or other every night so the job was essentially great for a bloke in his twenties. Everything else in my life looked set, too. I was in a serious relationship with a girlfriend I loved. I had bought a flat and could very well have settled down and made this my life. But I looked into the future of married life, kids, a steady desk job and I just knew I didn't want that – not yet, anyway. I wanted to travel, I wanted adventure; I wanted to be accountable to no one. But try telling that to your parents and your friends who value security more than you do – they thought I was insane.*

Working with my coach, I literally picked a city – Hong Kong – and decided I was going to go there on such-and-such a date and planned my resignation. The coaching helped me identify that travel-guide writing would be the ideal profession for me, but at that point I was more intent on just making the leap.

Maybe I was scared that I wouldn't do it. The thought of spending the rest of my days in London always saying 'I would have liked to have travelled' became unbearable to me. Just resigning and getting on a plane was a great way of making sure I made the leap. You then have no choice but to make your new life work.

And I had my work cut out. I arrived in Hong Kong, one of the most expensive cities in the world, with almost no savings in the bank and with no firm work lined up. If someone had told me what my first year would be like, I probably would have been too scared to do it. That first year became a lesson in how little you can actually live on. I lived on £7000 but still managed to travel to Cambodia, Africa and China (twice). I based myself in Hong Kong and lived in this beautiful shared apartment on the beach. Although I never seem to have any money, I never woke up dreading the day ahead.

If you're having trouble motivating yourself to make the leap out of your old life, set it up so that not doing it is more painful than actually doing it. I told everyone what I was going to do, set a date to fly off, set a date to resign and set up business meetings for when I got there. If I had bottled it, I would have felt very foolish. I know it's a cliché but sometimes you do have to 'just do it'. Leap now and worry later, I say.'

Baby Step 2:
Meet your Inner Pessimist

If we see light at the end of the tunnel, it's the light of the oncoming train.
Robert Lovell

Whether you've tortured yourself with visions of loneliness and alcoholism or you have gently resisted the picture of a traditionally 'nice' life, you have hopefully now motivated yourself to jump out of the water. You haven't boiled to death but you're standing there dripping, getting cold and probably feeling scared, and a touch weepy.

And this is where you'll get the dubious pleasure of meeting your Inner Pessimist. I say 'meet' but you're probably very well acquainted with your Inner Pessimist already. He or she is always there, at every crossroad in life, hovering in the wings. You've made the biggest decision ever: you've decided to leave your career and company car behind to explore India or you've decided to leave your diaphragm in the cupboard to try for a baby or you've decided to leave your wife and home to discover yourself. The truth is that you're leaving the struggle behind to live a delightful life; you're leaving the warmth and safety of what you know to start something new and you're scared, but you're going to try anyway. 'Oh, you don't wanna be doing that...' says the Inner Pessimist. 'What have I got to lose?' you ask yourself. 'Everything', shouts your Inner Pessimist.

If only the Inner Pessimist lived in the real world. Then we could tell him to mind his own business, blowing him a loud raspberry and offering a two-fingered salute to make our point clearer. But the Inner Pessimist doesn't live on your street, he lives in your head.

When you've come out of denial, you're in a very vulnerable position. You need lots of encouragement, hand-holding and acknowledgement. Your Inner Pessimist knows this and this is exactly when he'll pounce. Your Inner Pessimist calls himself a realist. 'But I'm just being realistic', is his favourite phrase. But don't be fooled – he's a pessimist in disguise and ready to dismiss, negate and pour scorn on your ideas and dreams.

Ten things your Inner Pessimist is most likely to say

- You're not good enough. I'd shelve this idea if I were you.
- You're a loser. Good try, but it's best to quit while you're ahead.
- You're really stupid! Whatever you do don't open your mouth.
- Really they all despise you and laugh at you behind your back. I'd stay in if I were you.
- You're fat, your nose is huge and you're funny looking. They would never fancy you in a month of Sundays so don't make a fool of yourself.
- You're completely talentless. Don't show anyone your work or you'll just humiliate yourself.
- They're rich and posh and you're common and poor. Never the twain shall meet.
- You might have hit a lucky streak but it will all go wrong soon. I wouldn't celebrate if I were you.
- You're poor, you're stupid and you're ugly – and you're thinking about doing what?! Oh, don't make me laugh. . .
- Your life is terrible because you are terrible.

MAKING THE BIG LEAP:
Salma Shah, 30, Big Leaping from IT sales to life coach and MD of her own coaching company

My Inner Pessimist is incredibly persistent and ultimately doesn't believe in me. He is very good at disguising this lack of belief into care and concern about my survival. 'What? Leave your lovely, well-paid job in IT? You want to become a writer and a life coach? There are hundreds of life coaches and writers out there – you'll never be able to compete.' He encourages me to always play it safe, not to take risks. He chips away slowly at my confidence if I try to do anything different. 'Salma, why are you wasting your time and energy doing this?' I find it so exhausting at times, especially when every inch of me was screaming to make a change.

Having initially drifted into IT, I'd managed to carve out a career that paid well. The first time I had the feeling of 'there had to be more', I moved to a company and got a higher salary. To my shock, the feeling of wanting more didn't diminish. Instead, it got much bigger. As the urge to make the Leap and re-train to become a coach and writer got stronger, my Inner Pessimist's voice got louder.

So what did I do? I stopped hanging out with negative friends who have a natural tendency to fuel my fears. I started listening to other friends, who said: 'There are many life coaches and writers, however, there is only one Salma, the life coach and writer.'

By listening to my Inner Pessimist, who always insists on comparing me with others, I set myself up to fail. By listening to my real friends, having faith and trust in myself, I was able to start my coaching training. If you want to pursue your dream, let 'faith and trust' be your mantra. And don't, whatever you do, listen to your Inner Pessimist!'

Many of us can live our lives thinking that our Inner Pessimist is the voice of truth because it plays such a huge, starring role in our head and shouts so loud that we don't think there's an alternative.

The good news is, there is, and we'll meet her in Step 2. For now, let's have some compassion for the Inner Pessimist. Difficult when he's swearing at us and calling us names, but we need to understand that the Inner Pessimist is just doing his job.

The Inner Pessimist thinks he's protecting you. Yes, he tends to go about it in a funny old way and yes, he does have a huge ego. Yes, he needs to be the one in control and yes, he needs to be overseeing everything, but generally it's because he thinks you haven't got a clue and he wants to help. The Inner Pessimist is like the worst ever parent you could have, the type that ill-advisedly tries to protect his children by telling them what to do all the time because he is certain that he knows better.

There is also a touch of self-preservation in there too. He doesn't want you to learn to think for yourself because we might fly his parental nest. He doesn't want to risk letting you get on with it yourself because then you might find you can do fine without him. In fact, deep down, I suspect your Inner Pessimist is terrified that you will do fine without him. That's why he fights so hard every day for his place in your life. And he fights dirty.

But I don't want you to fight him (he'll always win). At this stage, I only want you to be aware of him, so you can identify his voice, style and script.

READY TO LEAP?
EXERCISE: MEET YOUR INNER PESSIMIST

Part 1: Give your Inner Pessimist a name and a character. Write a description of him. Does he have dyed hair, an orange tan and a thin lipped smile? Go to town and really flesh him out. How does he speak? In high pitched tones, in a dull monotony or in a vicious rant?

Part 2: You're probably very familiar with the script that your Inner Pessimist generally uses. Answer the following questions in your journal. (Read the examples over the page to find out what Kate's Inner Pessimist said to her.)

- What is the pessimistic script, which keeps me stuck and feeling incapable of change? (Be specific – write the script in great detail.)
- How does that script serve me? (e.g. 'It allows me to torture myself so I keep myself small, which means I don't have to move out of my comfort zone, make a commitment to anything new or risk getting hurt.')
- What does it cost me? (e.g. 'I feel unbearably miserable. It costs me true success.'). To inspire you to dig deep, read Kate's script.

Kate's internal dialogue

'You're not lucky. Some people seem to get everything they want, it just lands in their lap. Not you. You're one of those people who is so talented in so many directions, but you're not up to surviving the cut and thrust of the real world. You're too sensitive, and you can never make up your mind which way to go. You're doomed to be hurt.'

'You couldn't hack it even if you succeeded. Ten, twenty years ago you had absolute faith in yourself, you were endlessly creative and you knew you could achieve anything. You didn't need a coach to help you keep yourself on track! But you've lost it! The world has eroded that faith. You've learnt that struggle is the way forward – people don't like brilliance. They're jealous and vindictive: they push you down. It's much easier to stay small.'

'People like you peak early – at school or university. You could make it in a small pond but not in the big wide-awake world. You work so hard for other people but when you're doing it for you, you just flake out. There are so many people who aren't that clever but they keep going until they're good at something. Not you, you give up at the first tiny hurdle, the first time someone hurts you. Hell! You can't even get up in the mornings. You're the world's worst decision-maker and you've got zero sense of direction. You're wasting your talents. You deserve to fail.'

How Kate's script served her

'It stops me from doing the real hard work that I have to do. It saves me from having to risk the disapproval of my family, who always wanted me to be a doctor. It enables me to hide behind the respectability of doing jobs and doing what I "should" do.' I'm always too busy doing a job or helping someone else to focus on what I really want. It enables me to carry on thinking that doing what I want is horribly selfish anyway.'

What Kate's script cost her

'My dreams. It causes me a lot of pain that I can repress for only so long then it comes back with a vengeance.'

Make a Little Leap

Calm down, calm down. If you're drinking coffee to get you going, eating sugar to calm you down and are always late (although it's never your fault) you're an adrenaline junkie. You may find it hard to keep to your goals as you're constantly overpromising and setting yourself up to fail by trying to cram too much into your life. Identify three triggers that give you the adrenaline rush and eliminate them. For example, if you're constantly late, leave 15 minutes early for every appointment, if you're constantly over-promising, deliberately underpromise regardless of the reaction you get.

Identifying the voice and script of your Inner Pessimist is essential for your Big Leap journey. Without that awareness, you will not be able to point your life in the direction you wish it to go in because, essentially, you are not choosing the way, you are letting your Inner Pessimist do that for you.

Your Inner Pessimist came into a starring role in your life during your childhood. His was the voice that kept you safe when you were a child. He was the one who would tell you how to behave or what to do to be loved and accepted in your family, in the playground and in the outside world.

He scanned the world for threats on your behalf and would tell you to 'be good', 'keep quiet', 'work harder', 'keep your head down'. If some-thing threatening happened, he would be the one to close down the hatches in your heart and mind so you wouldn't get hurt again.

For example, if someone teased you in the playground, your Inner Pessimist would help you draw conclusions about the world, like 'don't be different, it gets you punched', to make sure it would never happen again. If you crowed with delight at teatime for getting top marks in maths and your dad told you not to get above yourself, your Inner Pessimist would have been the one to nod sagely and suggest that if you wanted to be loved, it would be better if you didn't shine too much or get too much attention.

Your Inner Pessimist was simply doing his best to keep you safe, loved and accepted. He was teaching you how to get your childhood needs – for love, approval, safety or whatever it was you needed at the time – well and truly met.

The problem is that you've grown up now. You're not a child any more and you don't need that kind of parenting. You can make your decisions about what is safe or not safe all by yourself. But because your Inner Pessimist is so familiar to you, you never question him or question his role in your life. Out of familiarity and habit, you now look to your Inner Pessimist every time you have a decision to make. ('Make the Big Leap? Don't be ridiculous, far too risky', he says.)

Your adult self thinks that listening to your Inner Pessimist keeps you safe because that is all you've ever known – up until now that is. You have not realized before that you have been building your entire adult life around 'fitting in' because of an emotional need that you didn't get met when you were five years old and found that Johnny Bailey didn't like you when you turned up in the playground 'trying to be different' in your 'poxy Parker'. Or maybe you've built a disastrous romantic life based on a decision that you made as a six year old that men wouldn't love you if you were clever at maths – or clever at anything at all.

Guided by our Inner Pessimist, we have all made decisions and created behaviour patterns as children in order to get what we needed at the time and to keep us safe. As adults, we're usually not even aware we have such needs or that we have made such decisions to get these needs met. In order for us to make the Big Leap, we need to be able to identify those needs and get them met in a healthier way.

Baby Step 3: Getting your Needs Met

There is only one journey. Going inside yourself.
Rainer Maria Rilke

Unmet emotional needs – for approval, security or control – can be very strong drives in your life, so unless you identify them here, in Step 1, you won't be able to identify what you really want in Step 2, because the pain of unmet needs will always win over what you want.

Having unmet needs feels like being permanently hungry: they make you feel irritable and snappy. If an unmet need goes on long enough, it can make you feel as if you are emotionally starving. However, when an emotional need is met you feel satisfied, content, relaxed and that all is well with the world.

It is much easier to start creating the life that you truly want when you're working on a metaphorical full stomach, otherwise you waste a lot of energy scouring the world for leftovers. And sometimes if you're so starving for your need to be met, like Kate – I'll come to her in a minute – you end up down blind alleys, rifling through bins for scraps. You definitely need to know what your emotional needs are if your Big Leap journey is going to be a pleasant and successful one.

Emotional needs, however, are not a popular concept in western society. The word 'needy' is usual spat out as an insult – the more 'needless' you appear, the more emotionally healthy you are perceived to be. But that's a dangerous concept to buy because unless you're some kind of enlightened being, you will have emotional needs. Deny your emotional needs and they become like hidden addictions. You will do anything to get your fix.

Like Kate, you might end up spending seven years studying and training to work in a profession you hate. I don't know whether you noticed it but if you scan Kate's script once again, you can probably spot her unmet childhood need that is still driving her life today. In her own words: 'It saves me from having to risk the disapproval of my family.' Indeed Kate went through her torturous seven-year ordeal to become a doctor because of her need for approval. But it was as a nine-year-old child that Kate decided that the way to be loved by her family was for her to toe the line and 'be good at sciences'. She recalls: 'I remember winning a painting competition and running home after school to tell everyone. But dad, a doctor, didn't even put his news-paper down. "Very good, Kate but concentrate on the sciences." was his only comment. I loved painting, but at the age of nine, I think I gently folded my painting away in a drawer and struggled on with my biology homework.' Her need for approval from her father had been running her life ever since.

The tragedy is that Kate didn't realize this before. After spending seven years qualifying as a doctor, all she knew was that she was desperately unhappy and drinking a lot. It's a common tale. Our unmet childhood needs snap at our heels waiting to be fed, getting more and more irritated and upset as we ignore them. For most of us, it's not that we are denying our needs – we're simply unaware that they exist.

Whether you work 16 hours a day to meet your need to be accepted by your boss or eat maggots on a trash TV show to meet your need for acclaim, you should never underestimate the heights of miserable or bizarre behaviour that you can sink to when trying to get your emotional needs met.

Practically every addiction is propping up an unmet need. If you find yourself over-eating, smoking or drinking, you are most likely trying to anaesthetize the pain of your unmet needs.

By drinking, Kate was trying to dull the pain of her unmet need for approval. One of the reasons why many of us find it difficult to stop our bad habits has nothing to do with the addictive quality of the substance itself, but everything to do with trying to avoid feeling the pain of an unmet need. It is kinder to yourself to stop trying to give up your habits until you finish the process of getting your needs met as it will feel much easier then.

Make a Little Leap

Get some adoration. What three steps can you take in the next week which will allow you to spend time with people who you adore and who adore you? If this means cancelling all the appointments you have with the people who drain you, waste your time and energy – so be it. Basking in negative energy will get you more of the same so hang out with the people who want nothing more than to love you.

Cherish me!

I'm convinced that I was finally able to give up smoking because I finally identified my need to be cherished – and got it met. Yes, I admit it. I have a need to be cherished – I don't just want to be loved, I want to be adored! But I didn't know this. Neither did my husband. He couldn't understand why I was devastated when he would bring me a limp bunch of flowers back from the supermarket on my birthday. But as I wanted to feel loved, cherished and adored, droopy pink carnations from the last bucket in the petrol station didn't hit the spot. I assumed this meant he didn't love me and would often go into a deep sulk that lasted for days and create such a fuss that he would have to tap dance and sing beneath my window for weeks afterwards until I was once again convinced of his love.

My husband told me later that he had begun to dread my birthday or any kind of anniversary. 'I couldn't do anything right', he grumbled. It was the same for me when it came to buying presents for my friends. I would spend time choosing and buying thoughtful birthday and Christmas presents for them because I wanted to buy something that they wanted. But I came to realizethat buying special gifts wasn't about what they wanted; that wasn't important, it was what I needed that mattered. I was just giving what I hoped to receive: special gifts to make me feel special. I learned that this is familiar with unmet needs: whatever you find yourself giving too much of is usually what you are emotionally craving for yourself.

My friends didn't know about my unmet need to be cherished (I hadn't known about it either, so why should they?) and so they could never understand why I was so frosty when they gave me a book token. 'But I thought you liked books', they'd cry. I knew I shouldn't be so ungrateful but I felt unloved and irritated because they hadn't spent the time thinking of some special gift to make me feel cherished. The sulking, the frostiness and the tap dancing could have gone on for years if I hadn't discovered how to get my needs fulfilled.

If Kate hadn't discovered her need for approval, she may have just started on another career with one eye on her parents' faces: 'Do they approve? Yes? Okay, I'll be lawyer then.' Kate doesn't want to be lawyer or a doctor but until she gets her need for approval met, she won't know what she wants.

Discovering your unmet needs

The needs-fulfilment process probably causes more resistance than any exercise in this book, so if you want to throw the book across the room after reading this bit, that's okay. You are even allowed to skip it, if you wish. Though, if you do, you'll discover in Step 4 of the journey what happens when we listen to our Inner Pessimist and don't attend to our unmet needs.

The four-step process to help you get your unmet needs met:

1 Identify some symptoms of having unmet needs.
2 Identify the unmet needs themselves.
3 Identify the source of the unmet needs.
4 Fulfil your unmet needs.

Yes, you can get your emotional needs met. It takes practice and it can make you feel very uncomfortable at first, but once you learn how to get your emotional needs satisfied you can get on with identifying what you truly want as opposed to what you need. This is an important distinction if you are to make the Big Leap. It does make your Inner Pessimist very jumpy, though, so expect a lot of barracking and noise from him.

READY TO LEAP?
EXERCISE: DEALING WITH YOUR UNMET NEEDS

Part 1: Identify the symptoms or triggers of your unmet needs. Most of the time we're not even aware that our emotional needs are driving our behaviour. We will, however, recognize when we're unhappy, depressed, irritable, sad, jealous, angry or feeling unloved or unappreciated. These feelings are the symptoms of your unmet emotional needs.

When you next feel a negative , ask yourself this question:

'At this moment in time, what is it I'm not getting that I need?'

Is it a hug, praise, respect, control of a situation, acknowledgement, approval, to be heard, security, inspiration, success, to be loved? Only you will know.

Part 2: Find the patterns to your unmet needs. If you are still not sure what your unmet needs are, look at the statements on the following pages and see if you notice a pattern emerging or if any of the descriptions of unmet needs triggers a reaction in you. If so, this will help you to identify your unmet need. Of course, there are hundreds of different needs, but there are some common 'groups' of needs too.

DO YOU ANSWER YES TO THREE OR MORE OF THESE STATEMENTS?
- I become tense when someone is late.
- I become annoyed by others' sloppy standards.
- I am a tidy and methodical person.
- I can get snappy with disorganized people.
- I like to have possession of the remote control

Possible unmet need: to be right, need to be perfect.

DO YOU ANSWER YES TO THREE OR MORE OF THESE STATEMENTS?
- I'm often tired because I'm rushing around helping my friends out.
- I know instinctively how to make people feel good.
- I make lots of effort to find out what is going on in the lives of friends and family so I can be there for them.
- I feel outraged and resentful if people don't appreciate me.
- I send thoughtful presents and cards to friends and colleagues just to let them know I'm thinking of them.

Possible unmet need: to be approved of, to be needed, to be loved, to be liked, to be cherished.

DO YOU ANSWER YES TO THREE OR MORE OF THESE STATEMENTS?
- When things are going well for me, I literally light up inside.
- I will work very long hours and pull out all the stops to ensure something is a success.
- I'd rather die than be a failure.
- I'm always aware how friends and colleagues are doing and can be quite competitive.
- I am great at achieving goals.
- I have workaholic tendencies – I feel tense inside if I'm not accomplishing what I set out to do.

Possible unmet need: to achieve, to be successful, to feel worthwhile, to be accepted.

DO YOU ANSWER YES TO THREE OR MORE OF THESE STATEMENTS?

- If I'm criticized or misunderstood, I sulk.
- People say I can be difficult and too emotional but I don't think there is anything is wrong with that.
- I know how to make a really big scene if I don't get what I want.
- Rules are meant to be broken.
- I tend to brood a lot about my negative feelings.

Possible unmet need: for acclaim, to be special, to be different, to be heard, to be understood.

DO YOU ANSWER YES TO THREE OR MORE OF THESE STATEMENTS?

- I'm an expert in my area.
- I love to study something in depth and really get my teeth stuck into it.
- I am the eternal student.
- I often lose track of time because I get carried with what I'm doing.
- I won't try anything new until I'm confident I know everything I need to know.

Possible unmet need: to be competent, to be the expert, to be capable.

DO YOU ANSWER YES TO THREE OR MORE OF THESE STATEMENTS?

- Anxiety is my middle name.
- I worry about everything, everybody and his dog.
- I like having a boss I can respect.
- I find it difficult to make a decision without asking all my friends, my parents and my colleagues first.
- It takes me ages to make a change to another job.

Possible unmet need: for security, for safety, for support, for certainty.

DO YOU ANSWER YES TO THREE OR MORE OF THESE STATEMENTS?

- I get bored easily.
- I'm curious about stuff.
- I love travelling and having fabulous holidays.
- I am all over the place most of the time – people think I'm a bit dizzy.
- I always feel like I'm missing out on things – the grass is always greener on the other side for me.

Possible unmet need: to be stimulated, to be free, to be satisfied.

DO YOU ANSWER YES TO THREE OR MORE OF THESE STATEMENTS?
- I like to challenge people – no-one could call me a shrinking violet.
- I tend to have huge temper tantrums.
- I am independent and don't like people trying to tie me down.
- I don't rely on anyone.
- I love trying to achieve the impossible.

Possible unmet need: to protect yourself, to determine your own way in life.

DO YOU ANSWER YES TO THREE OR MORE OF THESE STATEMENTS?
- I'm one of life's peacemakers – I can't bear a scene.
- There's no point dwelling on the negative.
- I like my home comforts.
- People tend to get too worked up about the little things – I can't see the point.
- I go with the flow.

Possible unmet need: for calm, for agreement, for steadiness, for peace.

Part 3: Identify the source of your unmet needs. As our unmet needs usually stem from childhood, travel back in time to your childhood and answer the following questions in your journal:
- As a child, what behaviour earned you 'brownie points'?
- As a child, what behaviour earned you disapproval?
- What decisions did you have to make as a child to survive and thrive in your family?
- How are those decisions showing up in your life now as an adult?
- What effect are the those decisions having on your life now?
- What decisions could you now make differently so you will be able to survive and thrive as an adult?

Part 4: Fulfilling your unmet needs. Once you have identified your emotional needs, it is time to work out a strategy to get them fulfilled – in a healthy way, rather than sulking or spending years studying to get the approval of your parents.

You'll need help from others to do this, although, ironically, we often unconsciously surround ourselves with the very people who can't meet our emotional needs. You will need to choose people who care for and love you enough to help you do this, so create your need-meeting team carefully. If you're struggling to think of a team, just choose one person.

- Choose a team of friends and family who would be willing to help you meet your needs.
- Explain to them about the concept of unmet needs.
- Choose the unmet need with the most symptoms you identify with, the one you recognize most easily.
- Create a Needs Fulfilment Project and give your team specific and measurable things to do or say to get your need met. For example, if you have a need for approval, get them to email you every day with another reason why they like or love you so much.

Kate was appalled when I asked her to create a Needs Fulfilment Project. In fact, she refused at first. It felt absolutely alien and ridiculous to her. 'I'm not going to ask people to approve of me. That's awful. It's false and stupid. And if I have to ask, then it doesn't count anyway.'

I agree that this exercise is very challenging. The problem with our unmet needs is that we assume people know what we need and are in some way choosing to withhold their love, support or praise. That's not the case, they simply don't know. (If they do know they are withholding it, you need to ask yourself why you are spending time with these people anyway.)

As my husband told me: 'I'm not psychic.' I've had to train my husband to cherish me. I literally wrote him a list of cherishing things he could do every week because he didn't know what I meant. So I got specific: I wanted him to leave notes under my pillow saying why he loved me, I wanted flowers, I wanted surprise emails telling me another reason why he loved me, I wanted surprise phone calls to let me know when he was thinking about me, I wanted notes on my windscreen telling me how much he fancied me.

My husband, a practical Yorkshire man, raised an eyebrow and said he'd try. He did: I have never felt so happy, so in love, so adored. Our sex life improved, I felt so loving towards him and much more open to listening and supporting him. It was a win-win situation. I felt expansive, loved and loving. I felt like a completely different person. My husband was delighted that he could finally do something right and, although it doesn't come naturally to him, he now knows how to make me happy because he knows what I need. So he doesn't have to put up with my sulking and he doesn't have to tap-dance and sing under my window to win me back any more.

I am convinced this exercise helped save my marriage when it was floundering. If I hadn't been given this exercise to do, I would have either driven my husband away with my sulky tantrums or made an assumption that he didn't love me and left the marriage. What that would mean is that 11 years on, I wouldn't be married to the most wonderful man in the universe, who is the father of my child. Needs fulfilment – it's life-changing stuff.

Kate was eventually talked into creating her own project. She wasn't being difficult when she refused at first. This exercise takes courage because it makes you very vulnerable. Kate said it would feel 'almost like death' for her to ask someone to help with this exercise. She was afraid her friends would either refuse or to say they would help and then not to do it properly.

It feels 'like death' because it asks you to risk having confirmation that the Inner Pessimist is right – that it is unsafe, that you are unlovable unless you do a, b, or c, that love is conditional, that you must protect yourself otherwise people will mock you. These are the hidden, and sometimes not so hidden, beliefs about ourselves that we have formed in childhood. We are going to tackle beliefs in Step 3. For now, it's enough to identify your needs-fulfilment team and try out this exercise.

So what happened to Kate? She did ask a team to help her fulfil her need for approval. Her sister, her boyfriend and her best friend were spectacular at cheering her on. Her boyfriend put up 'You're amazing!' banners in her hall, her sister emailed her every day for a year with 'another reason why I love you' and her best friend dedicated 10 minutes a week to telling Kate why she was so special. Perhaps this is why she is currently working as a locum as she finances herself through art school. Once you have your needs fulfiled, you can do what you want, rather than twisting yourself into a career or life that you don't want in order to get what you need emotionally.

'I'm not sure where it's going to lead me but I know I want to spend some part of my life creating and painting. You never know I might use my medical degree and put it all together and do some art therapy?' Kate cried when she told me what her dad had said when she told him she was going to art school. 'I never knew you were so unhappy, Kate. I thought medicine would give you the start in life it gave me. I just wanted you to be happy. Do whatever makes you happy.' Kate told me: 'The greatest thing is that I'm happy NOW even though I haven't worked out exactly what I want to do. I feel as if I can do anything. I am ready to paint the town red – maybe literally!'

What your Inner Pessimist is probably saying right now:

'Big leap? More like a Big Heap! Don't listen to any more of this drivel. Put the book down and go and watch the TV instead. This author is obviously insane. It's not denial, at all. It's simply reality. That's just how life is. And if you ask anyone to help you with that needs-project thing, they're going to think you're weird. I think it's better for everyone all round if you put this book down now. Whatever you do, don't turn the page.'

What you need to be doing right now:

Thanking your Inner Pessimist for his contribution – but turning the page to find out what it is you really want in your life. After all, that's why you're here, isnt' it?

Take Ten Baby Steps

When you're overwhelmed, take these steps to get into action:

1 Ask yourself how you can simplify your life in the next three days e.g. stop watching TV, cancel social arrangements, order take-out for every meal.

2   Once you've bought some space, ask yourself: 'How can I eliminate three big projects from my life e.g. resign from volunteer groups, forget redecorating (get the experts in) and stop parenting adult children.

3   Hire a cleaner. Or anyone else who will help free up your time so you can do something more interesting.

4   Hire an accountant. Clear the path to understanding your money so you can handle more in your life.

5   Write a list of 50 things you're 'putting up' with – from bobbly bed sheets to a boss' snide comments – and tackle each one or more over the next 50 days.

6   Remember that all change takes place in the present so create a 'power hour' – 60 minutes where you write a list of things to do and then get to work right now.

7   Make 10 decisions today. Non-decisions create emotional and physical clutter.

8   If the way is not clear – ask better questions.

9   Give up. If creating something requires massive amounts of effort and struggle, it's likely that you shouldn't be doing it.

10 Do the task you're most dreading first. The rest will be easy.

Big Leap Step 2:
Identify what you do want

'I want a life I adore.'

You can have anything you want if you want it desperately enough. You must want it with an exuberance that erupts through the skin and joins the energy that created the world.
Sheila Graham

Congratulate yourself because you've done the most challenging bit and you've only just started!

You've taken your first step and started your Big Leap journey. Having met your demons in Step 1, you now know what they look like and you can deal with them. You can leave Victim City behind, shelve that Misery Interview and treat your Inner Pessimist like the over-protective parent that he is.

It's time to play, to start enjoying the journey and begin to think magically so you get what you really, really want. Get your wand out, let's create some magic!

Big Leap Step 2: Taking the Baby Steps

1 Getting out of the Void of Fear
2 Meet your Inner Coach
3 The Golden Glow
4 The Bingo Moment
5 Create the vision

What you're probably thinking at Big Leap Step 2

- 'Is it really possible to have what I want?'
- 'I'm scared but I'm excited.'
- 'This is just self-help psychobabble – it's not really possible to change.'
- 'But I don't know what I want.'
- 'I can't have an extraordinary life because I'm not extraordinary.'
- 'I want it all!'
- 'I can have it all.'
- 'Who am I kidding? I'll never escape this life.'

What you're probably doing at Big Leap Step 2

- Going to work, going through the motions and surfing the Net exploring 'a few ideas'.
- Daydreaming of a different life when you're off-guard.
- Telling your best friend about a new idea you've had.
- Watching TV or reading books about people who have changed their lives.
- Writing a five-year plan.
- Spending the millions you are going to earn when you get to your goal.
- Laughing a lot more – before being plunged into despair.
- Hiring a coach.

Big Leap Step 2 is where the birth of your dreams begins. Once the fog of denial has cleared and you are motivated to change, and once you have started to get your unmet needs satisfied, you can start to work out what it is you really want.

Generally, we all know what we don't want but identifying what we do want is often much harder. You may glibly say: 'I want to win the lottery' because we assume money will make us happier (of course, it might help), but after you've travelled the world and sun-bathed on a Caribbean beach for eight weeks, and after you've played with your new cars, clothes and accessories and decorated your new house – what happens next? If you've got a to-do list as long as your arm, you might be more clued up than some, but you still need to get in to action. If you haven't got a to-do list at all, then you probably need to find out what you want to put on it before you think about making your Big Leap.

You may not know what you want to do with your life at this point. Your future plans may be no more that a glimmer but right now, you need to keep that glimmer alight. This means making a decision.

Baby Step 1: Getting out of the Void of Fear

Without knowing how or if it's right – you need to make a decision that you are going to find another way to work, live and be.

This decision will light the way in the darkness and you will need that glimmer of hope and faith to be able to see your way forward. We need a touch of magical thinking here. Darkness and misery can be scary but they can also be great places to hide. When you light the match, you're scuppered – because then people can see where you are. You can't hide any longer. Are you willing to come out of hiding?

A word of caution: if you decide to hide for very long, you'll end up in the Void of Fear. This is where you go when you've come out of denial – you've decided that you really don't like what's going on in your life and you're going to change – but before you've begun to develop your dreams you have one discouraging conversation or read a piece of unexpectedly negative information, and you simply give up and get trapped in the Void of Fear.

'I can't find what it is I want to do/nothing is inspiring me/I'll just stay with what I know', you wail. Instead of moving forward, you teeter on the edge of possibility but you hide from the light – after all, that brightness just makes the world seem even more terrifying than before. A whole new life is beckoning but there are no guarantees and there is no certainty. It simply feels like you're in a void and if you don't fill it with faith and hope, it fills with fear instead.

MAKING THE BIG LEAP:
Lynne McNicoll, 47, Big Leaping from being a housewife to running her own Virtual Assistant business

The Void of Fear was horrible for me. I knew something was wrong with my life but I just felt I was stuck with it. I had not worked for seven or eight years and knew I was withdrawing more and more, even from friends. I felt I wasn't even a good friend to be around. I was bored and boring. I hated myself for not doing anything about my boredom, my fitness, or being overweight.

My 'glimmer' was an article in The Sunday Times *I read about coaching and that's when I thought I should hire a coach. Even then it took me weeks to call to start the process. I was scared of trying something and failing. What if I was crap at this as well as everything else I did?*

I felt I had a huge hand holding me back, telling me I was useless, telling me I deserved to be fat and bored. I was so ashamed of myself I wouldn't go out with my partner to business events because I felt I looked awful and had no personality and would let him down. He never thought that and was so sad that I thought it.

I knew that if I started the coaching, my life would probably change and I was scared of that too. I knew I 'had' to change, to do something, but I was terrified. Committing to the coaching was a Big Leap in itself for me. I was committing to myself, I was committing to change, I was committing to taking baby steps to a new life. One year on, I feel happier, more relaxed. The hand is still there but the hold it has is very loose and I hope one day to lose it altogether.

My advice for anyone to get out of the Void of Fear is stop procrastinating and just do it! I hung around far too long there and it's agony. You can change your life, you can get out of the Void of Fear – just do it, you're one baby step away!

The Void of Fear

The Void of Fear is where your Inner Pessimist is strongest. It's the only voice that you can hear. It can be all-consuming, so huge – and so paralyzing that it not only stops you in your tracks, it stops you from doing anything. You can end up living in the limbo of the 'out of denial' phase, hating your life, feeling disappointed with yourself but doing nothing to change it. It's a horrible place to live and some people can spend their whole lives living there.

What it feels like to live in the Void of Fear

- Hopeless. 'I'm stuck here.'
- Energy sapping. 'I can't be bothered.'
- Gut churningly envious. 'Look at them with their perfect, smug lives...'
- Miserable. 'I hate my life, I hate my life, I hate my life.'
- Sad. 'I've wasted my life.'

Grace strikes when we are in great pain and restlessness ... Sometimes at that moment a wave of light breaks into our darkness, and it is as though a voice were saying: 'You are accepted.'
  Paul Johannes Tillich

Every day that we stay in the Void of Fear, it gets worse. All we can hear is our Inner Pessimist going on and on at us. It can be exhausting. We go back to the jobs or relationship that we know instinctively is wrong for us and try to make it right, trying hard to make it work. We come away feeling like we've been wrestling with a sabre-toothed tiger every day. He hasn't eaten you yet but he might do tomorrow.

The Void of Fear is also the place where envy loves to live. You look at other people with happy lives and are filled with a green, mean-spirited envy – you hate their clothes, their cars, even their happy children. You smile and nod over the garden wall but secretly you want them to crash and burn – for him to lose his job, for her to get fat and ugly and for the kid to turn into a toad or vandal.

The Void of Fear is not a pleasant place to live. So put yourself out of your misery. Leave it behind and take a trip to La-La Land – the happy zone.

Make a Little Leap

What is really draining your energy? Putting up with rubbish in your life holds you back – be it needy friends, the junk in your cupboards or the junk food in your diet. It's time to get clear. Make a list of three things you are tolerating at home or at work – then blitz that list TODAY.

Living in La-La Land

Living in La-La Land? There are several names for this particular land mass. There's 'cloud cuckoo land', 'get your head out of the clouds, you silly bugger' continent, 'she's off with the fairies again' island. I'm sure wherever you were brought up, you'll have your own version. Whatever yours is called, it's time to decide to take a trip to this strange and distant land, so leave reality behind and have some fun.

For once in your life, you don't have to 'get realistic' or listen to the Inner Pessimist because you are simply going to daydream. When you daydream, your Inner Pessimist tends to go to sleep for a while because he doesn't feel threatened by flights of fancy. Visiting La-La Land is great because you get to create your life exactly as you want it to be. You can be ostentatious and live it large with your dreams. Best of all, you can dream outrageously!

What would your life look like if you really went to town? See it, smell it and really go for it. There are only two rules: first, you must never wonder how you are going to do it for real (that's not allowed); and second, anything goes – you can move to a different country or even fly to the moon, if you wish! Your vision of La-La Land must make you laugh out loud, and feel exhilerated and slightly bashful. For inspiration, do this exercise.

READY TO LEAP?

EXERCISE: DESCRIBE YOUR TRIP TO LA-LA LAND

A journalist from one of the biggest and highest-selling magazines in the land is coming to interview you. You are living your La-La Land life. Write your answers in your journal.

1 Why does such a prestigious magazine want to interview you? What have you achieved?

2 Read the description the interviewer has written about your lifestyle.

3 How does the journalist describe you? What are you wearing? How old do you look?

4 The journalist wants to know about your love life and family life? How do you describe it?

5 The journalist wants to write a paragraph about your average day – paint her a picture.

6 Describe the big highlight of the year for you. How did it make you feel?

7 On your journey to achieving all you have in La-La Land, you've had some 'crunch' moments, when you've made decisions that got you to this place – what were they?

8 If you to were to give one piece of advice to your readers, what would it be?

9 The journalist asks you about your vision for the future. What is it?

10 The journalist asks what kind of legacy you would like to leave behind? What is it?

MAKING THE BIG LEAP:
The La-La Land vision of Big Leaper Nicky Hambleton Jones

I am being interviewed by The Sunday Times Style *magazine because I am fronting my own television series about Tramp2Vamp!, my styling company. The programme is spreading the message that you can transform yourself and raise your self-esteem by changing your look and your clothes.*

My big highlight this year is winning Business Woman of The Year for creating such a strong brand from nothing in such a short amount of time. I'm being bigged-up as the female Richard Branson. I'm not just a dolly bird fronting a TV show – I'm for known my pioneering business brain.

The TV series has been a massive success, which helps promote my

Tramp2 Vamp! products – we have everything from makeup to hair products. I spend three days a week working on my business and spend the other four with my gorgeous husband and two kids – one boy, one girl. We're all very healthy. I'm looking particularly fetching today in just simple jeans and a white tee-shirt to show off my tan! Today we've just got back from our villa in Tuscany where we usually spend six weeks of the year.

My husband interrupts the interview to kiss me and tell me our nanny, who helps out four days a week, has just arrived and he's going out and can he borrow my Audi TT, which is parked outside our four-storey house in Clapham, London.

We're all very excited about next year when Tramp2 Vamp! will hit New York and we are experimenting with a new line of accessories. The legacy I'm leaving behind? I want to be an inspiration to every woman out there who has low self-esteem – I want to show her that you can transform your look and your life. I want to be seen as someone who has walked my talk – to show that you can live your dreams and you don't have to compromise.

I hate to admit it, but I've fooled you – because your La-La Land vision is probably the nearest you'll get to how you REALLY want your life to be. Without having to listen to your Inner Pessimist droning on about getting realistic, you can dream really big without having to edit yourself. Nicky's La-La Land vision is quite spooky even for me to read – and it is very inspiring. When she wrote this vision, she had moved out of her flat and was staying on friends' floors: she needed the income from her flat to survive financially because she had just been made redundant. Nicky was also single. Nicky created this La-La Land vision with her tongue firmly in her cheek. Three years on, she's in the process of creating her global brand Tramp2Vamp!, has her own TV series, 10 Years Younger, in the UK on Channel 4 and has just launched her own make-up brand. She's also in love. Be careful what you wish for, indeed.

If she hadn't had the safe space of La-La Land to dream in and had been asked to set some specific goals instead, I wonder if Nicky would have dreamed so big? Maybe. But her Inner Pessimist would also have leapt into action, screaming and shouting things like:

'Don't be ridiculous, you'll never do this in a month of Sundays' and 'Whatever you do, don't tell anyone – they'll think you've well and truly lost it.'

Baby Step 2: Meet your Inner Coach

I truly believe that we should never give up on our hopes and dreams. The path may be rocky and twisted, but the world is waiting for that special contribution each of us was born to make. What it takes is courage to follow those whispers of wisdom that guide us from the inside. When I listen to that, I expect nothing more than a miracle.
Marilyn Johnson Kondwani

If we are to make the Big Leap, create the vision and really attain all that we are capable of, we need to start listening to another voice. My clients have many different names for that voice – from the voice of reason to the voice of God – but I call her the Inner Coach.

No matter what you call her, most of you will have heard her whispers. (The bad news is that she is softly spoken so the whispers can be difficult to hear). I suspect she's the one that's been nudging you recently, telling you that 'there is another way'; perhaps she even persuaded you to pick up this book. For you to make the Big Leap, it is her voice that you need to be able to tune into. She is the one who will champion your dreams, tell you to have faith when all seems dark; she's the one who'll send help when it gets tough.

Ten things your Inner Coach is most likely to say

- 'You don't have to do anything to be loved.'
- 'You are smart, beautiful and funny.'
- 'Whatever happens, no matter how this turns out, you're going to be fine.'
- 'Oh, stop taking it all so seriously. In 12 months from now you won't even be able to remember what you were worrying about. Smile.'
- 'You have many gifts – when are you going to start using them?'

- 'It's normal to doubt yourself. Have faith. You'll be okay.'
- 'What are you learning here?'
- 'Hold my hand, take a deep breath and now stop. You don't have to do anything to be accepted. Just be who you are.'
- 'When are you going to start having some fun?'
- 'Go on, I dare you, make the leap.'

If we're serious about being able to hear the wisdom of our Inner Coach, we need to learn to meditate. Finding some quietness and being able to observe your thoughts for five to 15 minutes a day is the fast track for making the Big Leap. Our Inner Pessimist is so loud and strong and has ruled us for so long that it can take quite a bit of practice to hear the soft tones of the other voice. Meditation helps. Firstly, it gives you a space to gain an awareness of both voices. (I don't know about you but when my Inner Pessimist gets all stoked up, I find it hard to separate his voice from reality. His predictions become my reality.) Meditation helps me to start realizing that it's just one rather loud, aggressive voice. And in the quiet, you can start hearing another voice, your Inner Coach, who has much nicer things to say.

The Inner Coach speaks from a different place. While your Inner Pessimist speaks in your head – a rattling, obsessive drone that takes you round and round in circles, going nowhere – your Inner Coach speaks through your body, not through your thoughts. She talks through your gut instinct, your feelings and your intuition. You cannot justify the messages of your Inner Coach through logic. You know you've heard her when you say: 'It's just a feeling you've got.' Or 'My gut feeling is telling me something.'

Make a Little Leap

Get specific about what you REALLY want by identifying three people you envy (only real stomach tightening envy will do) in the major areas of life - career, body and relationships. What is it about their career/body/relationship that you covet? Are they writing a novel, or having great sex? Do they have effortless gym routine and a lean body with sexy legs? Envy is a great wake-up call to help you discover your unexpressed goals and dreams.

Ten ways to tell when your Inner Coach is speaking to you

- Your decision 'feels' right.
- You 'just know' that this is the right path.
- You are very clear about what it is you want.
- You feel relaxed and happy about your decision.
- You feel like you're in 'the flow'. Coincidences start happening. 'You'll never believe it . . .' Is your favourite phrase.
- You feel a flicker of excitement in your stomach.
- You trust your intuition even though you have no evidence to back it up.
- Even though life doesn't look as if it's necessarily going in the right direction, you know it is.
- You find yourself inspired with ideas more often than before.
- You begin to trust your decisions.

MAKING THE BIG LEAP:
Salma Shah, 30, Big Leaping from IT sales to life coach and MD of her own coaching company

You need to 'tune in' to your Inner Coach. You have to get really still – literally. Spend time on your own, whether you walk round the park or lock yourself in the bathroom. Then ask yourself: 'What am I feeling?'

My Inner Coach talks to me through my gut feelings. When something is right for me, I feel very calm, very sure. When it's not right for me, there's a lot of confusion, lots of trying to persuade myself in my head. Recently, I went for a meeting in London, where I was invited to put on a series of workshops. It was a fabulous opportunity on paper but my gut feeling told me to walk away. My head was nodding but my stomach was in a knot. There was something about the woman who was telling me about the workshops that didn't feel right. I just didn't pick up a good vibe from her. Logically, I can't back up my decision to walk away but I just 'knew' it was right. You can try and persuade yourself all you want that this is the right thing to do but if you don't get that good feeling, then forget it. You will save yourself lots of time and energy in the long run.

EXERCISE: HAVING TEA WITH YOUR INNER COACH

Part 1: Imagine you've invited your Inner Coach for tea. What does she look like? Does she have angel wings, is she dressed in white or does she wear jeans? How does she speak? How do you know that she is speaking? How do you feel in your body when you hear her words?

Part 2: You're probably not that familiar with the script of your Inner Coach. The Inner Pessimist is such a bully that your Inner Coach usually gets drowned out. If you're unfamiliar with her script, create one now in your journal. If she were to speak, what would she say? How do you know your Inner Coach is speaking to you?

- When you're afraid – what does your Inner Coach say? (Be specific – write the script in great detail.)
- When you feel you're not good enough, what does your Inner Coach say?
- When you feel ugly, what does your Inner Coach say?
- When you feel sad, what does your Inner Coach say?
- When you're exhausted, what does your Inner Coach say?
- What script would you have to hear to create the life you really want? (Write this script in great detail.)

Meet Kate's Inner Coach

'You are so amazingly creative, you just need to learn to trust yourself and your talents so you can do more of what you love. When you really believe in yourself 100 per cent you get everything you want. It is truly possible to believe in yourself like that every year, every day and ALL THE TIME. Forget what other people think; it's only when you trust your own judgement that you do the right thing for you. You've had so many extraordinary achievements. A lot of people would be glad to have done half what you have: like getting millions of A-grades and a degree from Oxford.'

'You've got loads of great friends and a rich, diverse and adventurous life. In fact, you always get what you want, when you want it hard enough – you just pretend you don't. Stop putting yourself down when you achieve beyond your wildest dreams, saying: 'It's not enough' or that you messed up on some piddling little detail. You're brilliant, talented, highly creative, beautiful and special, and you deserve to get absolutely everything you really and truly want.'

If I'm going to do all this, it will mean I have to listen to this voice – the one that says I'm brilliant and fab. The one that tells me to believe in myself and build up evidence to believe in myself. The one that says I can have everything I want and more. That way I'll be contributing the most to the world and giving the most back to those I love, too.

Baby Step 3: The Golden Glow

Be yourself; no base imitator of another, but your best self. There is something which you can do better than another. Listen to the inward voice and bravely obey that. Do the things at which you are great, not what you were never made for.
Ralph Waldo Emerson

Listen to your Inner Coach more frequently and the world will become a different place. You can begin to create a way of working, living and being that truly works for you. Even more important, you can identify what you really, really want. The problem is that you've probably been listening to your Inner Pessimist for far too long, in fact, so long that you've probably lost touch with what you want.

Most of us had our childhood dreams kicked out of us years ago so we have no idea what we really want to do with our lives. At some point our teachers, parents or friends have told us to get a grip; that we'd never be an astronaut but had we thought about accounting? Most of us, at some time or other in our lives, were told to 'get real'.

It's no good blaming our parents or teachers, though. They thought they were doing the best for us. They lived in a world ruled by their own Inner Pessimist. 'It's a tough old world out there and you'll get awfully disappointed with silly dreams like that', they said.

We believed them and learnt to override the championing of our Inner Coach. We fell into step with a world ruled by its Inner Pessimist. We ended up with a grown-up life, thinking: 'How did I get here? This is not what I want.' Or 'This is great, but something is missing.' But because we don't know what that is, we keep our heads down and just hope it will get better.

In this part of the Big Leap process, we're going to dig around and start getting you back in touch with what you do love, what you do enjoy and what does make your heart sing. I call it Golden Glow living and it is the way we live our life when we listen to our Inner Coach.

To live in the Golden Glow, you need to work out what you really want from your life, what makes you happy and what you value most. Here, you can measure what works for you and what's right for you by checking in with your emotional compass, rather than with a tick-list of 'shoulds'. You'll know when you're there because life will feel completely right; you will be able to make decisions with your hand on your heart saying 'yes, this is right' and those decisions will be based on what makes you feel good about yourself and not on someone else's rules.

The truth is most of us grew up living our lives by someone else's rules, playing the roles that society demanded we played in order to be 'happy'. We passed exams, launched ourselves on a career then bought the car and the house to go with them. We did all the 'right' things, lived by all the 'right' rules. Now, though, we can't understand why we're not happy and why we are so desperately resentful and exhausted.

To live a different kind of life, you have to start living by your own rules and rediscover what you want for yourself. It's time to create your own new rulebook; your very own touchstone for life.

Ten signs that suggest that you're living a life based on someone else's rules

- It takes you hours to make a decision (because deep down you haven't got a clue about what you really want or what's really important to you).
- You often end up doing things you don't want to do and resent doing.
- You always search for an 'expert' to help you – you never trust your own instincts.

- You appear to 'have it all' but still feel something is missing.
- You envy enthusiastic and passionate people – what are they getting so excited about?
- You feel directionless.
- You dread going to work every day but you do it because it pays the bills.
- You hate going clothes shopping because you don't know what suits you.
- You find yourself bitching and gossiping about other people because it makes you feel better about your own life.
- You're surrounded by people who bitch and gossip about other people. (You're often scared that if you leave the room, then they'll be bitching and gossiping about you.)

To create the Golden Glow, you need to design and build your life upon your values. When you do that, you will feel the 'Glow' and create a life for yourself that will feel magical and deeply fulfilling. Do the following exercise and write your answers in your journal.

READY TO LEAP?
EXERCISE: THE GOLDEN GLOW

Look back over the past week (or month or year, if you're struggling) and remember ten golden moments - moments that you loved, moments that gave you a warm fuzzy glow.

Part 1: Identify the fuzzy moment and what you were doing.
Part 2: Write down what it was you valued in that moment.

MY TOP FIVE GOLDEN MOMENTS

Golden moment 1: Waking up and not having to do anything I don't want to do that day.
What do I value? *Space and freedom.*

Golden moment 2: Coaching a client and connecting deeply with that person. I also love talking to my friends.
What do I value? *Connecting on a deep level with people.*

Golden moment 3: Watching inspiring films, listening to inspiring tapes, and reading inspiring books.
What do I value? *Inspiration.*

Golden moment 4: Learning how to scuba-dive.
What do I value? *Learning to master something new.*

Golden moment 5: I love brainstorming and coming up with ideas for articles/books and magazines.
What do I value? *Creating new ideas.*

My values are:

1 Space and freedom.
2 Connecting with people.
3 Feeling inspired.
4 Learning to master new things.
5 Creating new ideas.

Now list your values in your journal.

Needs vs Values

When they are first introduced to the concept of Golden Glow living, many people get confused between unmet needs (see Big Leap Step 1) and values. So what's the difference between a need and a value?

The short answer is that our values are what we are naturally attracted to doing when left to our own devices. We don't need to be motivated to 'get inspired' or 'learn new things' about what we value – we just want to. We CHOOSE to build a life around our values.

On the other hand, our needs are like urgent emotional cravings – we feel we have no choice but to get them met. We are DRIVEN to get our unmet emotional needs met, while our values are based on what we really, really want to do.

- Values are what your Inner Coach rewards you when you listen to her.
- Unmet needs are the fuel your Inner Pessimist uses to create fear and desperation.

Ten ways to recognize a value

- You look forward to indulging yourself in activities that are orientated around your values – you don't need to hire anyone or need anyone to motivate you to do them, you just do.
- If it's something you value, you'll probably have done it as a child. So, if creativity is one of your values, you will have written short stories in your spare time and if entertaining is one of your values, you will have tapdanced for your aunties.
- A value is something you are naturally interested in – it's the specialist magazine you'll always buy and look forward to reading.
- It could be a theme that runs through your life. So if 'freedom' is one of your values, you might have a freelance career and travel a lot.
- You feel fulfilled and relaxed, not driven and anxious.
- You'll having a Golden Glow moment when you do it.
- A value is something you do sooner rather than later.
- It's something you're naturally good at.
- You're not trying to prove anything to anyone.
- You feel happy when it is fulfilled.

MAKING THE BIG LEAP:
Andrew Stone, 32, Big Leaping from journalist on a trade magazine to Lonely Planet travel-guide writer

While everyone else wanted to settle down, I had this deep-seated fear of living a 'groundhog day' life – every day the same. I always knew I wasn't happy in an office, but it wasn't until I identified my values and needs that I understood why. My top two values in life are adventure and fun. I have a need for freedom but not for security.

That's why I am at my happiest travelling in a tiny town in Madagascar with £2.50 in my pocket – enough for the bus fare and breakfast – travelling on a wing and a prayer. Once you've identified your values and needs you can then set goals that will actually make you happy, rather than goals that you think you should set to please other people.

Baby Step 4: The Bingo Moment

Okay, so you've had a glimmer, you've left the Void of Fear, you've have a wild old time in La-La Land, you're getting clear about what gives you that Golden Glow – so now what? I'm hoping that you'll get the Bingo Moment soon and I suggest you do nothing until you do. The Bingo Moment literally hits you between the eyes. When it happens, you'll think: 'That's it! That's what I want to do with the rest of my life.' You'll feel alive, excited and so revved up, you'll want to dance up and down on the spot with glee. The Bingo Moment is when you find a career or some type of work, that will earn you money, that is orientated around your values.

I had been a journalist and knew it wasn't making me happy but I didn't have a clue what I wanted to do next. I had always wanted to be a writer – I thought that was my dream – so when I retrained to become a writer and found out that it wasn't, I was really stuck. I had hired a coach but no matter how hard I looked to find a new path, nothing inspired me.

Then, the week before Christmas, I was interviewing an expert for an article on how to survive the Festive Season and thought, 'Oh no, this is the same tired, old advice. I could do better than this.' Then Bingo! 'Oh my god. Yes! I could do better than this. I could train to be coach.' Even though I had been working with a coach, it had never occurred to me that I could become one. In that moment, I knew that was what I wanted to do. It was like a lightning flash. The next day, I enrolled on a course and stumped up the cash for coach training.

Looking back, I can see that all roads led me to coaching – like the voluntary work I'd done as a mentor (and enjoyed so much), my interest in human psychology (which had led me as a journalist to interview some of the biggest gurus of our time), and my fascination with self development. Also, I had hired a coach in the UK long before it had been popularized and I was deeply impressed by the sustainable results I had achieved. I also had the evidence for myself that it worked as coaching was one thing that had improved my life in a very long-lasting and also dramatic way.

So here was something I completely believed in, that was

orientated around four of my five values: connecting with people, freedom (I could run my own business and work from home), inspiration and learning. Now, I'm writing about it so I'm now fulfilling my fifth value of creating new ideas. Bingo!

All these thoughts came afterwards, but when I had my Bingo Moment I just 'knew' what the next step was going to be for me. It's a powerful feeling and for you to make the Big Leap, it's important that you have that feeling too.

Ten signs that you're having a Bingo Moment!

1 You feel sick with excitement.
2 You ring all your friends and say: 'You never guess what I'm going to be/do?'
3 You scream 'Eureka!' in the bath.
4 You wake up very excited and go straight to the computer and start writing and researching.
5 You don't do any work at the office because you're too busy surfing the Internet for information.
6 You start ringing round colleges, training organizations or estate agents so you can find out all that needs to be done to make the leap.
7 You start noticing other people on the train, start reading articles or start seeing things on the TV and radio that all confirm you're doing the right thing.
8 You ring up your best friend a dozen times a day because you want to talk to someone endlessly about this.
9 You wake up, remember your Bingo Moment and feel a smile splattered over your face.
10 You feel impatient and raring to go – your sights are fixed firmly on the future and you become very critical of the life you have now.

Let's do some digging

We sometimes have to dig around in our past to find some clues about what to go for before you get your Bingo Moment. Don't dismiss anything that comes up. Don't get into practicalities, either. Many of us see a glimmer: 'Well, I quite liked short-story writing as a child' but then dismiss it far too quickly: 'I can't change profession to be a writer at this stage!' so that we don't give ourselves permission to explore the idea thoroughly.

Just answer the following questions in your journal as truthfully and fully as possible, without editing yourself, and see if any themes or patterns begin to emerge.

READY TO LEAP?
EXERCISE: DIGGING FOR YOUR BINGO MOMENT

- What was your childhood dream before everyone told you that what you wanted to do was 'unrealistic' and to take your head of the clouds?
- Who did you viciously envy recently and why? Envy is a great tool to tell us what we really want – what have they got that you want?
- What are you naturally good at – what do you do effortlessly?
- What do you love doing? When you are doing this, does time slip past effortlessly?
- Is there anything you have seen on the television or read about in a magazine or newspaper that stirred your interest?
- What are you passionate about?
- What did you love doing as a child?
- If you didn't have to prove that you were good enough, what would you do with the rest of your life?

Still stuck?

You can't force your Bingo Moment. But if you've got to the end of the chapter and still haven't found your passion or developed a clear vision of the life that awaits you, don't panic. The bad news is there isn't a specific route to getting to the Bingo Moment. You don't fill in questionnaire A, Bingo Moment form B and personality test C and get your bingo. It's more organic than that. However, the first step is that you must be willing. If you are willing to be open to what the next step is for you, you start to receive some answers. You simply have to ask. What we focus on expands, so as soon as we ask a specific question, we will start to see, hear and feel the answers.

EXERCISE: LISTENING TO THE WHISPERS

1 **Write the question:** What are you trying to find the answer to? Think carefully. You can make the question specific e.g. What is the next step during the next three months? Or you can make the question big e.g. What is the purpose of my life? Whatever your question, write it down and then place it in one or two (or ten) places where you'll see it every day.

2 **Be willing to hear the answer:** You may see something that inspires you, a friend may start talking about something that makes you feel a rush of excitement, someone might just ring up and offer you a job.

3 **Feel it, know it:** There is no ambiguity about the Bingo Moment. You feel it and it feels right. There's no 'Ooh, I'm not sure about it'. Your Inner Coach usually tells you straight away. If you're still humming and haa-ing, then keep asking the questions and asking for clarity. Have patience: sometimes it doesn't happen overnight.

4 **Follow the whispers:** Remember that your Inner Coach talks in whispers and talks through your feelings and body, so it could be something subtler. Start noticing any kind of clues about how you're feeling. Any feelings of excitement, a skip of joy, any slight rush of emotion. Turn round and look at it, focus on it and turn up the volume by asking: 'What is exciting me here? What is it about this situation that makes me happy?' If you don't get an answer immediately, just keep asking the questions.

MAKING THE BIG LEAP:

Donal Doherty, 28, Big Leaping from bar manager to Director of Egoscue Method in London

If you want to discover what you are passionate about in life, you have to follow your feelings. I began to pay attention to things that I enjoyed, such as sport. When I was younger, I wanted to be an athlete. I had also become very interested in holistic approaches to wellness having experienced acupuncture, with great success. But 'lightening' didn't strike until I read Pete Egoscue's first book. When I had the opportunity see him speak in the US, I remember my stomach churning with excitement.

The Egoscue Method has been around in the States for 30 years and is endorsed by people such as golf legend Jack Nicklaus and best selling author Deepak Chopra. I just 'knew' that here was a golden opportunity to impact people's lives massively and to create a business around something I was passionate about.

This Bingo Moment didn't happen overnight. I had to follow the signposts of what 'felt right', to be willing to be open and trust that the path would become clear. When I first came to coaching, my vision was to become a therapist or coach and create a business around that. I had so many interests I wasn't focused. It was only by listening to my gut feelings that I knew I had found what I was l ooking for in the Egoscue Method.

My advice is to only do what you know feels right. Explore all the things that you were passionate about as a child and notice what you really enjoy now. Read books and go to workshops or talks by people who inspire you. Sometimes you have to work at it to get your Bingo Moment but it's worth it in the end.

READY TO LEAP?

EXERCISE: WHAT ARE YOU TRYING TO PROVE?

Creating a new way of living, working and being means focusing on enjoyment, fulfilment and inspiration. It means letting go of fear, struggle and having to 'motivate yourself'. You no longer have to prove anything to anyone. You are simply getting on with doing what you love.

One great way of testing whether this is truly the right path for you – and whether you are motivated by your unmet needs or your values is to ask yourself the following three questions:

- Could I spend the next five years doing this because I genuinely love doing it?

- Would I do this even if I wasn't paid to do it? (Not that I'm suggesting that you do.)
- If I had nothing to prove to anyone, would I spend my time following this path?

Baby Step 5: Create the Vision

Whatever you do, or dream you can, begin it. Boldness has genius and power and magic in it.

Goethe.

Once you've had your Bingo Moment, it's time to get serious with your La-La Land vision. The journalist has gone home but she's asked if she can come back tomorrow with a film crew tomorrow to film your ideal day. In your journal, describe what the viewer will see in your life-in-a-day documentary.

READY TO LEAP?
EXERCISE: A LIFE IN THE DAY

- Where do you wake up?
- How do you wake up?
- What's the first thing you do when you wake?
- Describe the people who are sharing your life?
- How do you behave around each other?
- What are you wearing/how do you look?
- How do you spend your morning?
- What do you do for lunch – where do you go/what do you eat?
- How do you spend your afternoon?
- Describe how you end your day?
- How do you spend your evening – with whom?
- What is the highlight of the programme?
- What message are you consistently giving out to the people around you?
- What impression is the viewer left with?
- What do people say to their friends about the documentary when they are discussing it the day after?

Make a Little Leap

Turn off the TV for a week You'll be astounded at how much time you suddenly create. If you settle down every night between 7-10pm to watch your favourite soaps and movies, you'd be gaining 21 hours a week - nearly a whole day just by making one finger movement on the remote control.

MAKING THE BIG LEAP:
Nicky Hambleton Jones, 32, Big Leaping from management consultant to celebrity fashion stylist and business owner

Think big when you write your vision. You don't have to know how you're going to get there. I always knew I wanted my own Channel 4 TV series and I wrote that in my vision but I had no idea how that was going to happen. I had absolutely no contacts in television. I was just a nobody with a new business, but in the end, the TV production company came to me. So when you write your vision, be bold. Don't worry about the 'how', just focus on what you really want to create for yourself.

Getting 'there'

This 'creating the vision' exercise comes with a warning. When we have a big vision, there is a danger that we live for the future and not in the present. We say to ourselves: 'When I get "there", I'll be happy.' We say: 'When I'm thin/famous/doing my dream job/married to my dream partner/got my novel published/live in Sydney/in my house in the country (you fill in the blanks), then I'll finally be happy.'

We learn this story from childhood fairytales. We watch our knights and princesses fight the dragon, marry the prince, transform the beast, go through their journey of struggle to get 'there' and then they all live happily ever after. But I don't want you to wait until the end of the story to be happy. I want you to be happy now.

This book is not about swapping one kind of struggle for another.

Why go to all this trouble to remove the struggle of commuting and living a life that exhausts you, simply to set yourself up to struggle even more to build our ideal life, just waiting for the day we can finally get 'there'.

If we have been attending to our unmet needs and we are building a life around our values and what we love to do, we can put this vision away. We don't have to struggle to create it, we don't have to set goals or motivate ourselves. We will simply be doing what we love to do and once we've identified what we want, our vision magically starts to fall into place. This explains why so many of my Big Leap clients achieve so much, so quickly.

The amount of struggle you encounter on your Big Leap journey is in direct proportion to the amount of time you spend listening to your Inner Pessimist, and whether or not you are attending to your unmet needs. (The more unmet needs you have, the louder your Inner Pessimist tends to scream.) The Big Leap journey can be a rich and satisfying one if you find your bingo moment, discover how to listen to your Inner Coach and live a Golden Glow existence. We don't have to wait until we get 'there' to experience what we want. We're there all ready.

What your Inner Pessimist is probably saying right now

'What a crock. I am so bored of this. You know this is complete crap, don't you? How are you going to survive living a Golden Glow life – whatever that means? What about the money, honey? You're going to give up your well paid job and do what? Become a massage therapist earning next to nothing – I don't think so! It really is just La-La Land. You can never do this in a month of Sundays – you know this, really, don't you? For God's sake, don't waste any more time or energy thinking about stuff like this – you're just going to make a massive fool of yourself. These Big Leapers – they're different – they've probably all got a trust fund to fall back on or they're just brainier and more talented than you. I admire you for thinking about all this but let's get real, shall we? Have you actually read your vision? C'mon, enough with the joking around. Good try but I think it's time you stopped fooling yourself. This Big Leap process is never going to work for you – you're simply not brave, talented or clever enough.'

READY TO LEAP?
EXERCISE: CALLING YOUR INNER COACH

Tune in to your Inner Coach. Write down in your journal what your Inner Coach has to say about all this.

Take Ten Baby Steps

10 baby steps to take when you need to be creative but feel about as creative as a block of wood.

1   Give up. Stop staring at the paper/screen and go take your dog/child/self for a walk.

2   Accept that you are feeling uncreative and do your taxes instead.

3   Every morning on waking, fire up your creative oven and write down 2 pages of nonsense, the first thing that comes into your head on a theme that you've thought of the night before e.g. blue, freedom, magic, your partner's snoring habit. It gets the creative juices flowing.

4   Listen to jazz. The Naropa Institute in Boulder in the US has found that jazz can lift the listener to theta consciousness – the highly creative brain-wave state associated with artistic and spiritual insight.

5   Invite round three friends for a creative brainstorm – play word association, ask questions like: 'How would your mother/boss/Tom Cruise tackle the task in hand?', ' What would inspire you to work seven days a week, 12 hours a day on your project?'

6   Go out, sit in a café with your favourite drink – whether that be red wine or cappuccino – and a pad of open questions to answer, such as 'What makes me feel excited about this project?', 'How many different ways could I do this?', 'Why do I want to do this?' And just start writing without lifting your pen off the paper. See what answers you come up with and be inspired.

7   Dance, sing, cook, paint with finger paints, sprint round the block and back, do impressions of John Cleese – do all or one of the above to change your mental and physical state.

8   Learn to meditate. Even five or ten minutes a day can help. A relaxed brain state contributes to heightened intuition and creativity.

9   Seek inspiration – go to art galleries, read inspiring quotes, listen to music that blows your hair back.

10 Give yourself an hour's breathing space. Often our creativity is blocked when we keep crossing out/tearing up our first attempts because 'it's crap!' Just let yourself create – write, paint, brainstorm – without editing yourself for at least an hour before you decide if it's any good.

Big Leap Step 3:
What do you have to believe to create the life you want?

If you believe that life's a bitch and then you die, you're right.

We are what we think.
With our thoughts,
We make our world.
   Buddha

If you want to change your life you'll need to change the way you think, the decisions you make and, most importantly, what you believe. What we believe about our life is our reality. If you believe the world is a harsh and cruel place, that's how it will be. But if you choose to believe that anything is possible and that all your efforts will be rewarded, then you'll experience that instead.

   In this step you'll identify what you believe, then you'll look at what you'd have to believe to create a reality that you want. Your beliefs won't change overnight, but if you decide to change your mind and take a different stance on some old beliefs you will find that life feels very different. That sense of ease will then be translated into how you approach your work, your social and family life, and your health to make a real difference to how you experience achieving your dreams.

Big Leap Step 3: Taking the Baby Steps

   1 What Colour is your Filter?
   2 What is the Cost of your Limiting Beliefs?
   3 New Belief – New World
   4 'I am a Sex God.' Acting 'as if'

What you're probably thinking at Big Leap Step 3

- 'I can't do this!'
- 'I've had a slight flight of fancy, now it's back to reality.'
- 'Who am I to think I could ever create this vision?'
- 'When have I got the time to even think about this?'
- 'Imagine if this was possible? But it's not so I better get back to reality.'

What you're probably doing at Big Leap Step 3

- Telling someone about your plans, seeing the look on their face and feeling incredibly foolish.
- Stammer when you say what you want to do.
- Tell people about the kind of life you'd like to create for yourself and then laugh uproariously as if you were joking.
- Stomp around feeling angry, saying: 'What the hell do I think I'm doing?'
- Isolate yourself – don't talk about how you're feeling to anyone, especially loved ones.
- Feel tearful, alone and like a mad person.

Brace yourself. Step 3 of the Big Leap process is where you actually get to make the Big Leap. Although if you are under the impression that making the Big Leap is about changing your job, or changing what you do, you may need to think again. Yes, things do change along the way but the real Big Leap is about changing what and how you think. If you want to change the way you work, live and behave – you need to start thinking differently. A Big Leap is a radical shift in thinking, which changes one or more assumptions we have made about our life. Once you've had a Big Leap then life will never be the same again.

So the good news (or the bad news, depending on how you see this) is that it's all in your head. Our thoughts and beliefs define our world.

What do you believe about yourself? What do you believe about life? Do you believe that life is wonderful, that you will be always be okay, that you are priceless, that you deserve only the best and that life is easy? Do you believe you will always be supported, that you'll always land on your feet, that life is fun, that you will always attract the best in life and that life is one big party?

Or do you believe that life is hard, money is the root of all evil, all men are bastards, all women are mad, life is a struggle, men don't commit, life is a rollercoaster, all men leave, all women cheat, and that you have to be a bad to be rich. Do you believe you'll never make it because you're not good enough, in fact you're actually pretty worthless, oh and you're stupid too?

What is your reality? What do you believe to be true about yourself and life? Because whatever you believe, you're right. The woman who believes that all men cheat and life is a bitch, and then you die is right. The man who believes all women are angels and life is a life long party is right too. They're right because they believe this to be true. Make the leap, change your beliefs and you can change your reality.

And if you don't believe me, ask the scientists. Quantum scientists and physicists such as Einstein have taught us that the physical body, like all material objects, is an illusion. Our world is simply what we perceive it to be. Reality is simply raw, unformed data waiting to be interpreted by you, the perceiver. We take a 'radically ambiguous, flowing quantum soup' as the experts call it, and use our perception to make sense of it. But our perception can be radically different from the next person's perception. If you take this thinking to its ultimate conclusion then you can change your world, your body and your life simply by changing your beliefs. Isn't that an exciting and liberating thought?

MAKING THE BIG LEAP:
Lynne McNicoll, 47, Big Leaping from being a housewife to running her own Virtual Assistant business

My old belief was: 'I'm not good enough.' I was surprised when I recognized that my belief went back to my childhood. Actually, not just surprised, I was also sad. How many years had I let slip by without grabbing opportunities? How much had this belief cost me?

Changing this belief has been a gradual process. With my coach, I agreed, that I had to change my focus – from only seeing evidence to support the view that I wasn't good enough to creating evidence to prove that I am.

It was a process of baby steps and big leaps. Baby steps included my very supportive partner writing out a dozen stickers with the word 'confident' on them and putting them on kitchen cupboards, doors, the tomato sauce bottle (!) and mirrors (there is still one on our bathroom mirror a year later and YES I look at it daily. I recognize how important it is to me!).

My big leap was starting my own 'Virtual Assistant' business. A 'Virtual Assistant' is like a PA but works for several clients at home. I wanted to go back to work again but I didn't want to back to the nine to five. My coach helped me identify what I was good at – organization, administration and looking after people – and I realized that I could create the perfect working environment for me at home. It was also the perfect 'belief building' environment. I would be doing things day in, day out that I knew I could do well, building my new belief that I was good enough.

Not that I don't wobble sometimes. The best fear-buster I've discovered is to write down any problem and break it down into manageable pieces. This works for anything from phone calls to fitness schedules.

Baby steps are the best way to create change. When I got terrified of phoning clients I wrote down step-by-step what I was going to say because when you're scared your mind freezes. Every time I take a baby step, it's one more piece of evidence I use to prove to myself, and the world, that I'm good enough. My confidence grows daily. You can take a baby step and then another and a year later you can see the difference and it's phenomenal.

Make a Little Leap

Just say NO! Just for today, resist temptation, say no to second helpings, buying clothes you don't need or losing your temper and be aware of how much control you really do have in your life.

Baby Step 1: What Colour is your Filter?

Whether you think you can, or that you can't, you are usually right.
Henry Ford

I think that beliefs are like filters: we fit them just behind our eyes and look through them at life. We are not born with our filters, rather we create them (albeit unconsciously) one at a time. As we go through life and slot them into place. We usually start with our parents' beliefs, then move on to our friends' beliefs, then the beliefs of our teachers, our peers, our employers, our society and our culture. We get to about the age of 21 (although some people say the process is complete by the time we are 10 years of age) and we have our filters well and truly in place. Our filter helps us make assumptions about how life is, how life will treat us, how to behave and not behave. They are usually totally unconscious: we simply assume that how we see the world is the way the world actually is.

When I first got my head around this, I felt my mind begin to melt. I realized that my beliefs are not the truth; they are not the way things really are. In fact, I had to face the fact that there might not be a reality the way I'd always understood it to be. 'You mean that I just made it all up?' I asked my coach. 'Well, yes', she said. 'Many beliefs are nothing but opinions that stay in place because we never get round question them. They become part of our subconscious and form the cornerstones of the reality that we experience – our worlds. We then validate our beliefs by selecting evidence that will support them, editing out anything else (in fact we may not even see it) that disagrees or challenges our beliefs, because it's too threatening.' That's why it usually requires a dramatic piece of evidence to 'shake' or change our beliefs.

Petra, a Big Leap client, lived her life with a very old filter in place – one that was 30 years old. She believed she was stupid. 'But you're a television producer', I said. 'But I've had to work so hard to get here and to stay here, you have no idea.' She'd say, scurrying off to work yet another weekend.

When Petra was six, she was kept down a year at school. 'From that moment on, I knew that I was the stupid one. It was so humiliating.' Petra had originally come to coaching because she didn't feel she had a life outside her job. She soon discovered her real problem was that she believed that she was stupid so she spent inordinate amounts of energy trying to prove to everyone she wasn't as 'thick' as she thought she was – a little game she had set up for herself since she had left school and got a first class honours degree at Bristol University! She worked very hard to prove that she wasn't stupid and when she got the accolades (the job positions that proved that she was anything but) she was terrified someone would find her out and discover her success was in some way a fluke.

Petra had plenty of evidence to prove that this wasn't true but because she believed she was stupid, she refused to see any other evidence to the contrary – until she started to look at beliefs and how they are formed.

Then Petra could see how she had locked herself in her very own self-made prison. She literally could pinpoint the moment when she formed her belief – it was when she experienced the horror and shame she felt at being kept down at school. She decided then that she was stupid and nothing could shift this belief. The belief formed and dried as hard as concrete at the age of six. At the age of 36, she still lugged this lump of concrete round with her wherever she went. Petra was horrified.

And it can be quite horrifying when we start to look at our beliefs and filters and see how they have negatively affected our lives. In fact, it's really easier to ignore this step. Perhaps you are thinking: 'Looking at my beliefs? I don't need to do that,' before you quietly turn the page. But that's just fear. Somewhere deep inside, your Inner Pessimist is pursing his lips and whispering: 'Somebody stop her – if she starts believing that she's good enough, we're going to be in deep trouble.' When you change your beliefs you are going to move out of your comfort zone quite suddenly and dramatically – and your Inner Pessimist will go to great lengths to prevent that from happening, all in the name of protecting you. So if you find that your Inner Pessimist starts shouting loudly at this point, just smile, wave, take a deep breath and be brave. For courage is needed for this next step.

Our old beliefs keep us in our comfort zone and keep us safe. If you believe life is hard, that men don't commit, that women are unfaithful, that no one really finds their dream career or that you're not good enough, talented enough or beautiful enough to create the life that you really want, you can avoid having to risk living to your potential. You know that if you do start living to your potential because you do believe you're good enough, you have to start taking risks: risks of failure, being wrong and, possibly, loss. So it takes courage to look at our beliefs.

Most of us are willing to look at our beliefs when our life doesn't seem to be working as well we think it should. So if you're suffering, it's a good indication that you may have some limiting beliefs in place. You just have to figure out what they are.

READY TO LEAP?

EXERCISE: WHAT DO YOU BELIEVE?

1   What decision did you have to make as a child to survive in your family?
2   What happens to people like you?
3   What will people say about you when you're dead?
4   What negative feeling do you experience most often?
5   When you get this feeling, what do you believe about yourself?
6   When you get this feeling, what do you believe about life?
7   What do you have to believe about yourself to have a career like yours?
8   What would you have to believe about yourself to have a relationship history like yours?
9   What would you have to believe about yourself to have a circle of friends like yours?
10 What would you have to believe about yourself, or life, for things to be exactly how they are right now?

Nicky Hambleton Jones, 32, Big Leaping from management consultant to celebrity fashion stylist and business owner

I had loads of negative beliefs kicking around. The main one was that I would never make it, that I was a 'loser'. I'd gone from job to job and I couldn't make it work so why on earth did I think my business idea would? I wrote all my negative beliefs on a piece of paper and realized how much unconscious energy I actually gave them. When I wrote them down, they did seem faintly ridiculous. So I created a new mantra: 'I am happy to succeed, I am happy to fail but I choose success.' I was embracing the failure because sometimes I was stressing myself out by running away from the idea of ever failing. But when I actually surrendered to that thought that it could happen, it took all the sting away.

Baby Step 2: What is the Cost of your Limiting Beliefs?

If you don't handle your neurosis, your neurosis will handle you.
  Chuck Spezzano

Petra was horrified when she identified the real reason she didn't have a life – i.e. she believed she was stupid and had to spend all of her life over-compensating to prove that this wasn't true. We can spend our whole lives trying to disprove something we believe about ourselves. We can decide in childhood that we're not good enough, clever enough or whatever, and then spend our whole lives compensating, trying to prove that we're okay. As you will discover in Big Leap Step 4, it is possible to create whole personalities as a means of compensating for our negative beliefs about ourselves. When we don't believe we're good enough inside, we will try all sorts of ways to show that we are on the outside but it will always feel like a hollow victory. Our cars, our clothes and our careers scream 'fake, fake,

fake' because deep down we feel we are pretending so the fear of discovery follows us wherever we go. We fear that if we didn't have our protective layer of possessions, careers and even body fat, we will be exposed.

It isn't uncommon for many of us to spend our whole lives running away from that fear of being uncovered as the useless loser or dunce that we believe we are deep down. And no matter how we dress it up – in Jimmy Choo shoes or a high flying career – we can't hide from ourselves the feeling of worthlessness we have inside. For many, fear is a great motivator – and the greater the fear, the greater the motivation to be successful. Through coaching my clients, I have discovered that sometimes the most successful people are the most terrified.

What is the price of success on this basis? If success is simply compensation for negative beliefs, anyone who lives in fear can never rest or be still – they must always be achieving. They will always want to get 'there' – to be thin, to be rich, to be happy – because they think when we're 'there' they'll be happy, that they can rest and that the fear will have gone away. What they don't realize is that the fear will never go away until they address what they truly believe about themselves.

Petra's belief about herself had served her well in that she had been very successful. Her fear of being found out had made her push herself to grand heights. But with a negative belief system like Petra's in place, she was always driven and always on the go because she could never be or have enough – because she could never feel that she was enough in herself.

So, like Petra, it may seem as if your negative belief system has been serving you well on some level, but in the end – if you don't face it – it will cost you more. This is why it is so tough to admit and come to terms with. Because, when you look at what a belief has cost you in your life, it can add up to frightening proportions emotionally as well as financially.

Petra realized her 'I am stupid' belief was costing her big time. She was so busy trying to prove that she wasn't stupid, she didn't have time to create a relationship – she was worried that time was running out and she wouldn't be able to have babies and her health was suffering as stress was aggravating her eczema.

91

Step 3: What do you have to believe to create the life you want?

'I'm a mess!', she wailed. 'And I'm stupid.'

'You are if you believe you are', I said.

'Not helpful', she snapped.

MAKING THE BIG LEAP:
Lynne McNicoll, Big Leaping from housewife to running her own Virtual Assistant business

My old beliefs have cost me dearly. I was emotionally drained and had left a good job years ago. I was simply unable to cope. I was also very overweight.

I felt like a doormat with my family ('Lynne'll do it'). I rarely refused because I thought it might buy me some brownie points. Funny that, it never did. In fact, I felt like I got even less respect. Even my partner, who had never wavered and had always given me full and unswerving support, could not convince me I was a really worthy person capable of much, much more.

My new beliefs have transformed my life. I have a career I love, with clients who are just amazing and inspirational themselves. I know change can and does happen. It has happened to me. I can do it!

I spent the first few months concentrating on my career. Then I added on my desire to improve my fitness. All baby steps. First I joined a health club then did one class a week, then added a trip to the gym. Last week I added another class so now I do two classes and visit the gym every week. As I get fitter I feel more confident. I can do it!

I feel I am now coming out of a shell that I have been building for years. I have met several new friends at my health club and the diversity they bring to my life is significant and welcome. I am seeing more of old friends who I had neglected (I had felt there was little point in seeing them as I thought they wouldn't be interested in me – would they?)

Where it is appropriate I can now say 'No' to my family and they don't seem to have suffered as a result! I now believe that I am more confident, enabled and empowered. I can do it!

And if I can do it, you can too. Go on, take a baby step.

EXERCISE: COUNTING THE COST

List your negative beliefs and for each belief, answer the following question in your journal:

- What this belief is costing you emotionally?
- What this belief is costing you financially?
- What this belief is costing you in your relationships?
- What this belief is costing you in terms of your health and wellbeing?

Baby Step 3: New Belief – New World

Things do not change; we change.
Henry David Thoreau

Petra didn't feel it was possible to change her belief. 'Whatever I do, I'll always feel thick,' she said resignedly. She believed she was different so she couldn't change the way other people could and that the process of changing beliefs wouldn't work for her. Another negative belief that kept her stuck.

At the beginning of this process it takes a massive leap of faith. How can you change a fundamental belief about yourself when obviously you believe it is distinctly untrue? 'How can I start believing I'm intelligent when, ever since I was six, I believed I was thick?' asked Petra. Good question.

Once you've identified your old belief, you need to replace it with a new one, one that serves you better. The way to do it is to decide on your new belief then find evidence to support it. After all, what you focus on expands. I discovered that it isn't enough to chant a new belief at myself in the mirror every morning. Affirmations are great, but to really make a new belief strong, it's important to start collecting evidence to really prove to yourself that it's true.

At first, it feels like you're trying to pat your head and rub your stomach at the same time. Having changed the belief, even if you catch yourself in the middle of an old pattern of thinking – 'I'm not clever enough' – you can now notice it and can decide to change it to 'I am clever enough' and support it with: 'I have a degree from Bristol University and I've just been given a promotion and I've just been given a Bafta', whatever makes it true for you.

It is good to look to past evidence to start changing your beliefs, but what I've found to be the most useful is to collect evidence every day and write it into a journal. Ask yourself to write five or even ten specific examples of why this new belief is true for you today. You're building evidence and as you change what you begin to focus on, your filter begins to change.

Experiment and play with this idea. Try the exercise below:

READY TO LEAP
EXERCISE: I BELIEVE ...

If you believed just one of these statements, how would it change your life?

Write in your journal how each belief would change how you approach your work, your relationships and your health.

1 I am supported and guided in everything I do.
2 My potential is limitless.
3 I'm not perfect but I'm lovely/great/wonderful.
4 Everyone is doing the best they can.
5 This too shall pass.
6 The present is exactly as it's supposed to be.
7 I embrace change.
8 I can learn from every situation.
9 I'm okay just the way I am.
10 I'm an attractive human being.

Christopher Gibbs, 34, Big Leaping from accountancy to becoming a student in media and psychology

Before I made the leap, I thought people were not supposed to enjoy work, just make money to survive. By writing down thoughts, thinking through issues and telling myself 'I can create the life I want' I managed to change my mindset and aim towards something I feel is truly worthwhile.

95

Step 3: What do you have to believe to create the life you want?

Baby Step 4: 'I am a Sex God.' Acting 'as if'

I am the greatest. I said that even before I knew I was. Don't tell me I can't do something. Don't tell me it's impossible. Don't tell me I'm not the greatest. I'm the double greatest.
  Muhammad Ali

Beliefs don't change overnight, so don't expect it to be an instant process. You have to be committed and persistent. But I believe it is one of the most life-changing processes you can ever commit to. Change a fundamental belief about yourself and you can change your world – without moving from your armchair. Well, that's not exactly true.

Our beliefs about life and ourselves form and then come true for us when we find evidence to support them. By acting 'as if', we start creating evidence to prove this new belief about ourselves is right. It can be incredibly scary as our old beliefs are still kicking around. But what we focus on expands. If you believe you've got no talent and you're going to fail, that's exactly what you'll create. But if you start believing and then creating evidence to support your new belief the momentum starts to build and your reality begins to change from the inside out. Play with this idea and have some fun doing this exercise.

EXERCISE: ACT 'AS IF'

By acting 'as if' you can quickly and rather dramatically adopt a new belief. Choose one of the options below and go and act 'as if' for the next week.

1 What would you do differently for the next seven days if you believed that you were the sexiest being alive?
2 What would you do differently for the next seven days if you believed you had the potential to create a business empire?
3 What would you do differently for the next seven days if you believed you were a creative genius?
4 What would you do differently for the next seven days if you knew you would always have enough money?
5 What would you do differently for the next seven days if you believed you were the most precious being on earth – more precious than your children, husband, best friend, parents?
6 What would you do differently for the next seven days if you believed you only had a week to live?
7 What would you do differently for the next seven days if you believed you would always have enough money?
8 What would you do differently for the next seven days if you believed your parents loved you?
9 What would you do differently for the next seven days if you believed you had a perfect body?
10 What would you do differently for the next seven days if you believed you were going to be given everything you ever wanted in the next year?

MAKING THE BIG LEAP:
Salma Shah, 30, Big Leaping from IT sales to life coach and MD of her own coaching company

It was the first time I had ever run a workshop and I was terrified. Terror is not a good look. So I decided to act 'as if' I had given hundreds of workshops before. Every night before the workshop, when I went to

*bed, I would visualize my audience loving my presentation. I would
practice it in my head. 'What would I do if I was a great workshop
presenter?' I asked myself. 'I would look great', I thought. I got into the
part and dressed like I knew what I was doing, then visualized it going
well, visualized people coming up to me afterwards telling me how
great I was.*

*Then I had the Big Leap in thinking. When I actually stood in the
shoes of an experienced workshop leader, I realized they wouldn't
actually be worrying about their presentation skills and desire to be
liked but whether they were positively influencing and changing the
lives of their audience. This wasn't about me; it was about them. I
realized that I wouldn't have all the answers but if a nugget of advice I
shared meant someone would walk out with a bit more confidence,
then my work was done. If I hadn't got into the part, and into the shoes
of that experienced workshop leader, I would never have made that
realization. The workshop went brilliantly after that.'*

Make a Little Leap

Fill Your Life Tanks: If you can't remember when you last took a
holiday, are constantly worried about money and drink a bucketful
of coffee a day to keep you going then your 'life tanks' are probably
empty. It is often difficult to set goals and stick to them until you
start filling those tanks. So, over the next week, select a 'tank' of
time, energy or space and find three ways of filling it until it's
brimming over. Then put a system in place to make sure it stays
that way. For example, if you want to fill your energy tank cancel
all social arrangements for the next week and go to bed before 10
pm every night. Then commit to having three early nights a week
from then on.

Awareness, awareness, awareness

So it's as simple as that then, is it? You identify your old belief, look at
what it's costing you, feel miserable for a while and then replace it
with a fabulous new belief, act 'as if' and you're sorted. Well, kind of.
I don't want to spread malicious rumours but sometimes it's not quite
as cut and dried as all that. Even after identifying my 'not good

enough' belief and replacing with a new, shiny 'I am good enough' belief, then building lots and lots of evidence to prove that this is true, I still sometimes feel terrible, useless and very below average. I have made my leap but I still fall flat on my face and splatter on the ground sometimes. Something or someone will trigger my old way of thinking and I will go straight back into the old – 'I'm useless, I'm going to fail, everyone is going to laugh at me' – script. The Inner Pessimist can be just as vicious these days as it could in the early days.

The difference now, though, is that I catch it sooner. I don't get into it as much. The old fear doesn't get branded into my nerves as much as it used to and I don't wrestle for days with that old miserable feeling. It may be just a few hours, even minutes, before I realize that it's just my 'not good enough' stuff rattling my cage.

And in the moment when I can observe it in its cage, rather than be in the cage with it, magic happens. In that moment, I can choose to hear another voice, I can choose to think differently, I can choose to make a leap.

I was comforted to hear Richard Alper (a.k.a. spiritual guru Ram Dass and author of *Be Here Now*) say that in 30 years of doing intense spiritual work, he has not let go of one of his neuroses. He is simply more aware of them. He can welcome them in: 'Well, hello, paranoia, I haven't seen you for a long time, come on in.' He is no longer paralyzed by his beliefs and he no longer gets engaged in emotional tussles with his neurotic thoughts, but is detached, watching them like interesting animals at the zoo.

The renowned meditation teacher and writer, Stephen Levine, talks about seeing our thoughts as boxcars on a freight train. He asks us to imagine standing at a railway crossing, watching a freight train passing by and challenges us to try to keep looking ahead into the present, rather than being pulled towards looking into each of the carriages: 'As we attend to the train, we notice there's supper in one boxcar, but we just ate, so we're not pulled by that one,' says Levine. 'The laundry list is the next one, so we reflect for a moment on the blue towel hanging on the line to dry, but we wake up quite quickly to the present once again, as the next boxcar has someone in it meditating and we recall what we're doing. A few more boxcars go by with thoughts clearly recognized as thoughts. But, in the next one is a snarling lion chasing someone who look like us. We stay with that one until it's way down the line to see if it gets us. We identify with that one because it 'means' something to use. We have an attachment to it. Then we notice we've missed all the other boxcar streaming by in the meantime and we let go of our fascination for the lion and bring our attention straight ahead into the present once again.'

I loved this description of the way our thoughts work while in meditation. But I also think it's a wonderful description of how our thoughts operate in general. Without the instruction or intention to keep our eyes straight ahead in the present, how many of us realize that we have a choice? How many of us remember that we can simply focus on another carriage – the one with the supper or the laundry list in it? Or simply focus on looking straight ahead into the present? How many of us realize that whatever we put our attention on can eat us up, whether it be a lion or a belief system? Negative beliefs are like snarling lions – they have us hooked. We are attached to them and we do focus on them and wrestle with them because we think if we don't, they'll eat us. The irony is that the more we wrestle and fight them, the more power we give them. However, to step outside and be able to observe our beliefs dissolves their power.

MAKING THE BIG LEAP:
Rachel Dobson, 30, Sunday tabloid journalist Big Leaping to freelance journalist and property developer

I am what is commonly known as a scatterbrain. Never play word-association with me as the random results can be too scary. Since starting to meditate I have freaked myself out further as I begin to explore how my mind can go from A to B via Pluto.

After leaving my job I set up my own business, but fell into the pattern of doing exactly the same stuff I'd always done – but because I worked from home I could do the washing at the same time! It was pointless. I needed to be still and take stock. Unfortunately, this didn't mean booking into a fabulous spa, it meant making a habit of doing absolutely nothing for a small part of each and every day.

I started going to a Hatha yoga classes at my gym – fantastic – lying flat on my back instead of pumping iron: easy. But the results are so much more obvious than spending weeks on the treadmill. The class has meditation at the beginning and end, and for me these are the most beneficial times.

As a beginner it's so tough to be still, but having the calming voice of a yoga teacher trained me into knowing how to relax and get into the flow of meditating.

At home I sit on my bed, propped up by pillows with a thick pair of socks on! Once I'm comfortable I concentrate on my breathing, in and out, gently through my nose. Every time I catch myself making a list of things to do that day, or having a chinwag with my bellowing old criticizing ego or Inner Pessimist (as Suzy calls it), I come back to my breathing. I reckon it takes, for me, a good 15 to 20 minutes to crack it. Around about then my funny, loving, calm big sis with lovely shiny, flowing hair – my version of the Inner Coach tells me everything's okay, you'll have a great day, you did as best you could yesterday, get out there and enjoy yourself, love.

At first I ended up in tears when all I could hear was The Bitch of an ego banging on. Now I hear her stampeding through and think: 'Hiya, come to have your say?' Then I go back to my breathing in and out.

When I open my eyes I feel refreshed, positive and focused. Then I let the good times flow, which they do. At the end of the day I take time to acknowledge the good things that have happened, too.

When I meditate in the morning, whatever happens that day, if I catch myself stressing or getting upset, I remember the breathing and that brings the feeling back. It's about me, what's happening to me inside and how I'm reacting to external things. I'm the only one who can deal with and control that, and I find my breathing is calming and helps me remember that. I don't sit cross-legged at my desk and hum, burn candles or play twangy mediation music. I just breathe in and out of my nose. It's like doing pelvic floor exercises, no one else knows you're doing it, you can do it anywhere and the benefits are magnificent!'

Levine's book *A Gradual Awakening* (See Suggested Reading for more information) is a beautiful book on meditation for beginners. Again, I recommend that you learn to meditate. Meditation will help you to step back from your negative beliefs and observe them, rather than constantly wrestling with your snarling lions. You can then CHOOSE to focus on your new positive beliefs or even choose to simply stand on the sidelines and choose to observe all your beliefs and thoughts, known in the business as 'just being'.

Make a Little Leap

> **Money talks:** If you were to save or earn an extra £100 – how could you do it? Work out three ways that will enable you to have a reserve of cash in your savings account in 30 days. From moon-lighting to spending an evening in the bath rather than the bar – be creative! Write down a list of your talents that you could make extra cash from or look at what you can sell. Could you work in a bar at the weekend for a month, have a car boot sale, sell your used books at Amazon or sell your old Beano annuals on an internet auction website?

Ten amazing facts about meditation*

- One study has found that a group of 50-year-olds who had been practising meditation for over five years showed a 12-year decrease in biological age.
- Research showed that meditation was the most effective way to shake off addictions such as alcohol and cigarettes.
- Studies show that meditation has been proven to increase attention span, perception, and memory while improving verbal and analytical thinking.
- Other studies on meditation have reported decreased requirements for medication among people who practise meditation including reduced use of sleeping tablets and anti-depressants.
- One study over five years found that among those who meditated regularly, there were 87 per cent fewer hospitalizations for heart disease, 55 per cent fewer tumours and 73 per cent fewer throat and lung problems.
- Many studies have shown that meditating regularly can reduce high blood pressure.

- Meditating consistently has also been proven to decrease emotional problems such as depression, hostility and aggression.
- An exhaustive study by the Swedish Natural Health Board found that psychiatric hospital admissions were much less common among people practising meditation than among the general public.
- Based on research and clinical experience, meditation has been proven to reduce stress-related disorders such as migraine and anxiety.
- In a controlled study on asthma, meditation was found to reduce the severity of symptoms.

*All the above refer to Transcendental Meditation, which has been proven to between one and half to eight times more beneficial to health than other meditation or relaxation techniques.

Cultivating awareness is the key to sustaining the Big Leap. The more awareness you have, the quicker you can catch yourself before you dive into your old negative scripts. Awareness means you are not at the mercy of unconscious thought patterns but 'at choice'.

Petra has learned to meditate. She now has a great deal of evidence to show that she is a bright woman and she now believes it. She believed it enough to resign from her job in TV and take time off to travel the world. She may come back to it, she says, but only if she decides it's something she loves. 'I have changed the way I feel about myself so I don't have to push myself any more. I feel like I have nothing to prove anymore. It's incredibly liberating. I've taken some time out to get back in touch what I want for myself but the door is wide open. I feel the world is my oyster.'

What your Inner Pessimist is probably saying right now

'Good grief! You'll be wearing caftan and sandals next. Be careful. This sounds really cultish. She'll be asking you to give all your money to Father Christmas in the next chapter, just you wait. C'mon, let's get serious. You can't honestly believe that meditation will make any difference to your life. What? Sitting down with your eyes closed? I think that's just a little excuse for a nap – don't you think that a tad lazy? And where are you going to find the time to do that? Time for a reality check, methinks. Put the book down now. How about a glass of wine? Or shall we go to the pub? So much more fun...'

READY TO LEAP?
EXERCISE: CALLING YOUR INNER COACHS

Tune in to your Inner Coach. Write in your journal what your Inner Coach has to say about all this.

Take Ten Baby Steps

10 baby steps to take when you need to move forward but are paralysed with fear.

1 Fill and empty your lungs right down to your belly 21 times, then ask yourself:'Who can I help right now?' Helping another in your moment of terror will put your issues into perspective and take the focus off what you think is a problem.

2 Remember that terror is a state of mind and it's a choice. Sometimes all we can control in life is our own attitude. Ask yourself: 'What is the leap in thinking I have to make right now?' Write it down, then ask your Inner Coach for help. You don't have to do it all alone with your Inner Pessimist barracking you. Meditate, tune in to your inner coach and ask for help. Say: 'Show me the way.' Then wait for the answers.

3 Focus on what is working. If you focus on what isn't working, you'll get more of the same. Identify three things in three areas of your life that work and do more of them e.g. You love spending time with your partner so organize an extra date this week, you love your yoga class so book a weekend workshop this month, you love reading – buy a new book.

4 Go back to basics and get a person who loves you to sit you down and tell you why you are fantastic as you are right now.

5 Make a list of 20 things you have achieved in your life that you are immensely proud of.

6 Stop focusing on the big picture and start cleaning up the details. Details occur in the present so you can do something about them without experiencing fear. Take three actions right now that will improve your life instantly – from having your hair cut to doing the washing up.

7 Make a commitment to a witness: 'I [name] commit to putting on my coat, getting in the car and at least driving to the venue.' It's harder to break a promise to others than yourself.

8 Get some perspective. Ask yourself: 'In ten years' time, will this even matter?'

9 Let death motivate you. Ask yourself: 'What do I want to achieve before I die? Will this next step be a step towards achieving my life's purpose?' No? Then re-focus. Take a step that will. If you're on the right road, there's only one way forward.

10 Face the fear. What is the actual worst case scenario? Begin by asking yourself: 'And then what would happen?' Then have a conversation with your fear:

FEAR: They'll reject the idea.
YOU: Then what would happen?
FEAR: I'll fall into a fit of despair and cry for a week.
YOU: And then what would happen?

FEAR: I'll realize that I'm a no-good failure and
   pine away.
YOU: And then what will happen?
FEAR: I'll die alone and unhappy.'

Fear is strongest when lurking under the surface of your
life. Shine a light on it and it generally shrivels. Try it.

Big Leap Step 4:

Scambusting

'Don't talk to me about Big Leaps, I've just found out my boyfriend is a woman.'

Often people attempt to live their lives backwards: they try to have more things or more money, in order to do more of what they want so that they will be happier. The way it actually works is the reverse. You must first be who you really are, then, do what you need to do, in order to have what you want.
   Margaret Young

Excuses, excuses. We can always find a reason not to do something, especially if it is challenging and difficult. But you've come so far, why stop now? You're in the process of changing your beliefs, you know what you want, so now is the time to go out and start making your new dream your new reality. This is where you can old behaviours can get in the way of your goal. I call them scams and they give us the perfect excuse – in our own view, of course – to hold ourselves back and not quite take the plunge. But I know that once you see your scam you can bust it – that's what Step 4 is all about: scambusting. Just do it. It's quite a lot of fun, so why not?

Big Leap Step 4: Taking Baby Steps

1 Identify your Scam
2 Understand your Scam
3 How to Bust your Scam
4 The Transition

What you're probably thinking at Big Leap Step 4

- 'Big leap? Big heap of crap more like.'
- 'I'm too busy looking after the children to focus on this.'
- 'I can't get my head around what I have to do.'
- 'It will all go wrong, it always does for me.'
- 'My husband/friend/dog has got a broken leg, I have to help them first.'
- 'I don't believe a word that is written in this book.'
- 'Don't talk to me about big leaps, I've just found out my boyfriend is a woman!'
- 'I have to finish writing this book/project/essay/email first.'
- 'My vision isn't detailed enough yet. Just let me get it right first.'
- 'Big leap into your bed. That's what I need.'

What you're probably doing at Big Leap Step 4

- Sneering.
- Sighing.
- Farting loudly and pointing at the dog.
- Giggling and simpering.
- Moaning.
- Flirting.
- Drinking coffee and smoking cigarettes.
- Shouting at people.
- Slapping strangers and flouncing out the room.

(If you don't understand, read on.)

You've come out of denial, you're working on your unmet needs, you've identified what you think you truly want in life and you've worked out what you'd have to believe to get it. Now in Big Leap Step 4, I want to stretch you a little bit more and ask you to leap a little higher. I want you to get naked.

You know that nightmare where you go out and suddenly discover that people are pointing and laughing because, in fact, you're stark naked and walking down the street in broad daylight? You know, the one where you try to run and hide but you always end up flashing your bum? (What do you mean – you don't have that dream?) Well, perhaps you will after reading this chapter because Big Leap Step 4 requires you to strip off a few layers.

Officially it's about uncovering your 'scams' but the process can feel like peeling off all your clothes on a busy street so all your goose-pimpled flesh is fully exposed to anyone who cares to look – which can make you feel rather uncomfortable.

What is a scam?

We create scams when we don't know how to get our unmet emotional needs satisfied in a healthy way and when our belief systems about ourselves and life are essentially negative. Scams are:

- A cluster of unmet needs and beliefs that have evolved into an 'identity' or behaviour pattern.
- A 'costume' we decided to dress up in when we present ourselves to the world, and perhaps even to ourselves.
- The emotional protection we created in childhood to help us survive in the grown-up world.

Our scams are essentially the systems we created to keep ourselves safe as children. The Inner Pessimist loves these kinds of systems. But scams can become very inefficient and, by the time we've reached adulthood, they're probably very much out of date. After all, when we are no longer children, we don't need a child's response to a situation.

As a child, you might have made a decision to become the class joker because you were bullied in the playground – the scam was useful then because it meant that the other kids laughed at you rather than thumped you. But 30 years on, behaving like the joker in the office is probably seriously holding you back. Your 'silly antics' might make people like you but they don't get you anywhere in your career.

So now it's time to decide to drop that old behaviour in favour of something more appropriate and reflective of you as an adult. If you need to, you can now learn some new ways to get your need for protection met – or maybe you can decide that you just don't need that protection any longer. After all, you're not in the playground any more and you can choose other ways to deal with any bullies you might encounter in your life. It's quite a liberating idea.

But let me tell you about my own little scam so you get an idea of how they work – or rather, don't work!

My little scam

My favourite scam used to be 'poor, brave me'. I was the world's favourite martyr. I did everything for everyone else – I was a giving friend, a dutiful daughter, and a wife who supported her husband emotionally (and financially) for a while. And how was I? 'Fine, if a little bit tired/stressed/worn out,' I'd say with a little sigh.

I'd set up this scam in childhood. This is how I got love and attention as a child. At some point I'd made the decision that love wasn't unconditional and I would have to do a, b and c to be loved.

The way I chose to get the love I wanted was by being a giver and a martyr. I would clean the house for my parents, I was the good one who wouldn't stay out late because I didn't want my parents to worry, I was the sweet, giving one of the family. I got lavished with praise, love and attention for playing this little scam. It was glorious. I was loved by almost everyone. Everyone would say how lovely I was. No one could ever criticize me or say anything bad about me because I was doing everything 'right', I was being there for everyone, was 'sweet and kind' and 'only trying to help'. I got what I needed. It was a fantastic scam to set up, even though I do say so myself.

However, 30 years on it wasn't working for me any more. I was twitchy with resentment. I was constantly screening my answering machine because friends were always ringing me to dump their problems on me. 'No one ever listens to me', I'd sigh. I resented my husband for having the freedom and money to go off and follow his dreams even though I couldn't follow mine; but I'd never say anything, I'd just stew inwardly. 'You go on, darling and be happy. I'll just sit here and be miserable.' I know, nothing so revolting as the smell of burning martyr, is there?

I'd find myself working all the hours because I didn't want to say no to my bosses. I wanted every one to like me and think I was incredibly hard working and dynamic. Predictably, I began to lose my energy. I started to use stimulants such as coffee and cigarettes to help me get through the days as I was constantly exhausted. Which meant I got to 'sigh' all the more, and yes, I still got to be a martyr but eventually, I was fed up with it. It was costing me big time – my relationship, my health, my sanity. 'Time for some scambusting', my coach suggested.

Baby Step 1: Identify your Scam

We have not passed that subtle line between childhood and adulthood until we move from the passive voice to the active voice – that is, until we stop saying 'It got lost,' and say 'I lost it.'
  Sydney J. Harris

Scambusting? We'll get to that in a minute but first let's take a look at some of the more popular scams that we play. There are hundreds of scams that we can play. And the first step is identifying the scam. It's not the most pleasant part of the book. Believe me, if you're normal, you don't want to own up to a 'scam'. To be honest, it's downright embarrassing. In fact, many people can get very angry when they read the descriptions below.

Some of us are so highly identified with our scam, we think we are our scam. If we stop playing the scam, then who are we? We will protect our scams at all costs because we feel our scams protect us. They are what we have constructed to emotionally survive our childhood and if we start wobbling that protection barrier, we can become very defensive.

It can feel frightening to suddenly see your scam in black and white. I was highly identified with my scam. I felt like someone had taken away my personality. If I wasn't the martyr or people-pleaser, then who was I? How would I react, how would I act, what would I do with the rest of my life? I'd been playing the people-pleaser since childhood – how was I supposed to behave now? Be prepared to react quite strongly when you read the descriptions of the scams. Listed below are some of the more typical scams that we play along with description of the possible unmet needs that they fulfill and the belief systems they may be trying to compensate for.

If your scam still serves you well and is costing you very little, then you probably won't find this section very useful. If for example, you have created the Joker scam and have made a career and a fortune from being a comedian, you probably won't want to start looking at this stuff. Your scam works for you still.

However, for those of us who are struggling, you may find the scams outlined pages on the following useful.

The scam: Playing the Cynic

Being cynical and sneering and disbelieving about anything other than what you think is right. A permanent sneer is etched on your face.

The most likely thing for a cynic to say: 'Yeah, right!'

The most likely thing for a cynic to do: Snort derisively.

Possible unmet need: Protection.

Possible pay-offs: It keeps you safe. You don't have to come out of your comfort zone – it's easier to sneer and mock other people's efforts than actually dare to do something differently yourself.

Possible belief systems you are compensating for: 'You can't trust the world. You can't trust life. You can't trust others.'

Possible costs: You find it difficult to create intimate relationships and you feel lonely. You make enemies easily. You're not that likeable, although some people think cynicism is cool so you may be popular in certain groups of people – like journalists.

The scam: Playing the Martyr/People-pleaser

You do everything for everyone else and quietly resent it. People generally take the Martyr for granted and do not feel grateful for the help they give.

The most likely thing for a Martyr to say: 'Don't worry about me.' Sigh.
'I'll just stay in and do that for you.' Sigh.

The most likely thing for a Martyr to do: Sigh quietly.

Possible unmet needs: To be loved/approved of/needed/feel secure.

Possible pay-offs: You make yourself indispensable in everybody's life so no one will leave you, you don't have to risk failing or coming out of your comfort zone because you spend all your energy sorting out other people's lives.

Possible belief systems you are compensating for: 'I am not enough. Love is conditional. I must do a + b + c to be loved.'

Possible costs: You're constantly exhausted, you become bitter and resentful, your children never leave home, you die never having achieved what you wanted to achieve.

The scam: Playing the Joker

You constantly laugh and joke and have everyone around you laughing all the time. You play lots of silly tricks at work and at home.

The most likely thing for a Joker to say: 'Have you heard the one about. . .?'

The most likely thing for a Joker to do: Fart loudly and then point at the dog.

Possible unmet needs: To be liked, to be safe:

Possible pay-offs: You never have to be honest about how you're really feeling and you never have to make yourself vulnerable. People generally like you as long as you don't take it too far and you're usually the most popular person in a group.

Possible belief systems you are compensating for: 'No one will love me if I'm just me. Everyone is a threat I need to disarm. I'll be attacked if I don't protect myself.'

Possible costs: You never get to talk about how you really feel and so you can feel lonely and isolated. People don't take you seriously at work – which can cost you financially as well as emotionally.

The scam: Playing the Flake/'the Blonde'

You play the dizzy Flake who just can't get her life together – you're usually in debt, have relationship traumas but you're almost proud of the fact. Family and friends smile at you indulgently.

The most likely thing for a Flake to say: 'Oh, you know what I'm like!'

The most likely thing for the Flake to do: Giggle inappropriately.

Possible unmet needs: Protection, to be looked-after, to be loved.

Possible pay-offs: You don't have to risk taking responsibility for your own life because you get looked-after by others and get lots of attention. You are usually greatly loved by others because you don't threaten them. People love to hear your 'disaster stories' because it makes them feel better about their own lives.

Possible belief systems you are compensating for: 'I must appear unthreatening to others or I will be attacked, I'm not clever/good enough/beautiful enough to get what I want, or I am clever enough/good enough to get what I want but if I show people that they will attack me so I'll pretend I can't do it so that I stay safe.'

Possible costs: Your life is in constant crisis, which can be pretty stressful at times, especially if you don't have your usual team in place to rescue you. If you want to live comfortably, you have to hook up with someone wealthy (parents or partner is usual) as you'll never be able to afford the good life on your own.

The scam: Playing the Misery

You're always unhappy and constantly moaning.

The most likely thing for the Misery to say: 'Life is hard and then you die.'

The most likely thing for the Misery to do: Fold your arms, turn your mouth down at the corners as you walk silently and utterly miserably away.

Possible unmet needs: To be nurtured, to be listened to, to be soothed.

Possible pay-offs: You get a lot of attention from people who love you because they want you to be happy as they are constantly trying to help you or make a situation better. You can get a lot of attention if you join a new group as they also can try to 'fix' your misery.

Possible belief systems that you are compensating for: I am invisible/will not be loved unless I have a problem.

Possible costs: Eventually people who love you get fed up with your moaning and may leave you. In a group situation, after being the centre of attention for a while, people soon lose interest as they realize you are determined not to be cheered up. You can become very unpopular and therefore isolated and lonely. (Hook up with a martyr or rescuer – see below – and this probably won't happen.)

The scam: Playing the Rescuer

You spend your life rescuing people or animals and generally focusing on lost causes and people. Usually you will be going out with or married to an alcoholic, depressive or Misery (see above). Generally you get more joy out of helping people than the Martyr (see below).

The most likely thing for a Rescuer to say: 'Let me do that for you.'

The most likely thing for a Rescuer to do: Tap dancing and laughing trying to make the person being rescued feel better.

Possible unmet needs: To be needed, to be loved, accepted.

Possible pay-offs: You always have a role to play in any group situation. You're generally respected and admired by others. You're seen as being a 'good' person. You receive the grateful thanks of your rescuers (if you are not thanked, you become a martyr – see above).

Possible belief system you are compensating for: 'My needs aren't important/I must always meet others' needs before my own to be loved and accepted.'

Possible costs: It can be exhausting. You tend to slump in a heap at the end of the day. You never have the time or energy to sort your own life out because you're too busy cheering up everyone else. So you're generally unfulfilled and dissatisfied with life. You worry constantly about others and how they are. You constantly ring people just to check they're okay.

The scam: Playing the Rebel

You hate any kind of authority and constantly rebel. You always hate your boss, whatever job you're in.

The most likely thing for the Rebel to say: 'Fuck 'em!'

The most likely thing for the Rebel to do: Light up a cigarette in a non-smoking area.

Possible unmet needs: To stand out and to control your own destiny.

The possible pay-offs: You feel special and different. You get a kick from not conforming, which can buy you admiration in some circles. You can be quite creative in finding new ways to do things (in an attempt to be different) so you could be very successful at running your own business.

Possible belief system you are compensating for: 'I am not special. If I'm like everyone else, I will disappear/not be loved/noticed.'

The possible costs: You're constantly battling or fighting with people or organizations, which can be wearing for you and those around you. You might indulge in things that aren't good for you health-wise – like drugs, alcohol, and unprotected sex – which can cost you greatly in the long run.

The scam: Playing the Victim

Something terrible is always happening to you. You're either being victimized, bullied, sacked, mugged, losing your purse, getting ill (again), being cheated on by your partner or being badly treated by your friends.

The most likely thing for the Victim to say: 'It's not my fault!'

The most likely thing for the Victim to do: Sit in a circle of people, shoulders drooping, cataloguing the horrors that have happened to you that day.

Possible unmet need: To be listened to, to be looked after, to be loved, to be soothed.

Possible pay-offs: You do not have to take responsibility for yourself and can be passive and wait to be rescued by someone else (although you resist the rescue with all your might). You get lots of sympathy and attention. You don't have to come out of your comfort zone and risk failing or rejection.

Possible belief system you are compensating for: 'People don't/won't love me and it's my fault – because I'm unlovable.'

Possible costs: You live your life in the twilight zone of misery. You never experience real joy. People eventually get sick of your misery and start to move away, wondering if you're either cursed or you're bringing it on yourself. You can be quite lonely.

The scam: Playing the Drama Queen

Your life is a constant whirl of dramatic scenes – huge fights with your boss, visits to the hospital with cancer scares which turn out to be in-growing hairs and constant high-drama in your love life. Your would-be partners always turn out to be gay or married or commitment-phobes.

The thing most likely for a Drama Queen to say: 'Oh. My. God. You will never guess what happened to me today?'

The thing most likely for a Drama Queen to do: Slap someone and flounce out of a room.

Possible unmet need: Attention, to be adored, to be acclaimed.

Possible pay-offs: You are always the centre of attention. If you're not there, people are always talking about you. You get a lot of energy and buzz from constantly living in this field of high-drama.

Possible belief systems you are compensating for: 'I am nothing. I am nobody.'

Possible costs: You never get real or lead an emotionally healthy life. You can't form good, stable relationships and so tend to be surrounded by fellow Drama Queens, Rescuers or Martyrs who will listen to your tales of woe and try to rescue you or sit and sigh silently, or offer to go and buy you a pregnancy test.

The scam: The Adrenaline Addict

Generally you're a procrastinator who leaves everything to the last minute. Everything is always done in a rush and with much suffering. You use coffee, cigarettes or drugs to give you energy and to keep you going.

The thing most likely for an Adrenaline Addict to say: 'Let's do it tomorrow instead.'

The thing most likely for an Adrenaline Addict to do: Drink ten cups of coffee a day.

The possible unmet needs: To be approved of, to be valued for who you are.

The possible pay-offs: You get a lot done quickly. You are very 'high-energy' most of the time and can be very dynamic and successful in your career.

The possible belief system you are compensating for: 'I am not good enough, I will fail and everyone will laugh.'

The possible costs: You can push yourself so hard you end up collapsing and being very ill. If you're using adrenaline as a source of energy, it's usually because you're doing tasks/a career that you don't enjoy so you have to force yourself to do it using adrenaline. Being an adrenaline addict, usually means you're not living the life you really want to live.

The scam: The Perfectionist/Control Freak

Everything has to be done to your very high standards otherwise it's completely wrong. You'd rather do it all yourself rather than let someone else mess it up for you. You're the boss who has to oversee every last detail or the mother who won't let anyone look after her child because of your exacting high standards.

The thing most likely for a Perfectionist to say: 'You're doing it all wrong. Give it to me.'

The thing most likely for a Perfectionist to do: Shout at people – a lot.

The possible unmet needs: Control, safety, to be right, to be in charge.

The possible pay-offs: You are indispensable. You are the one always in control so you don't have to trust others. You can control your environment and it makes you feel very safe and secure.

The possible belief system you are compensating for: 'I have to earn my place in the world. This is the only way this can be done otherwise I will get hurt/attacked. I can trust only myself.'

The possible costs: You have to work 18 hours, seven days a week and it will cause you to burn out. You will never be able to take time off unless you're ill. You are the boss from hell and everyone will hate you as you don't encourage people, just criticize them. No one can do it as well as you can do it, so you have to do everything in your company or home.

The scam: Playing the Vamp/the Stud

You play the sexual lothario/temptress in every situation. You cannot finish a sentence without a double entendre. You seduce and manipulate people with your sexual wiles.

The thing most likely for the Vamp/Stud to say: 'I just can't stop staring at your lips.'

The thing most likely for the Vamp/Stud to do: Stare at your lips.

The possible unmet needs: To be noticed, to be in control, to be liked, to be loved.

The possible pay-offs: You have a role to play on every occasion and because you know how to charm and seduce people, you can be popular with strangers. Your self-esteem is regularly massaged – as is your body.

The possible belief systems you are compensating for: 'I am unlovable, I have to make them like me before they are able to reject me.'

The possible costs: As you get older, you become more unpopular and 'sad' as you cannot seduce with your looks any more. If you're rejected, you can quickly become very unhappy. You constantly have to move on to new groups of friends as your only way of communicating with people is to seduce them and once you've seduced everyone in the group, you have to move on to pastures new. This can be unsettling and isolating. You may indulge in unprotected sex and put your health at risk.

Make a Little Leap

Explore your home town. Pretend you're a travel journalist who will have to write a glowing write up of all the wonderful things to do in a 3 mile vicinity of your home. Check out local cafes and research the local history of the area. Looking at old sights with fresh eyes helps us appreciate what we have, rather than always looking at the horizon for something better. Yes, you want to achieve your goals, but appreciating what you have now will help you to enjoy the journey.

Baby Step 2: Understand your Scam

It doesn't interest me what planets are squaring your moon. I want to know if you have touched the center of your own sorrow, if you have been opened by life's betrayals or have become shriveled and closed from fear of further pain. I want to know if you can sit with pain, mine or your own, without moving to hide it or fade it or fix it.

Oriah Mountain Dreamer

You may not entirely identify with any of the above but you may recognize echoes of your behaviour or scam in them. Don't fall into the trap of pointing out to your friends and family what scams they're playing. You might think it's the perfect party game but it isn't, trust me. Just focus on yourself.

MAKING THE BIG LEAP:
Rachel Dobson, 30, Big Leaping from Sunday tabloid journalist to freelance journalist and property developer

If you really can't see the scam you've got running and you're feeling brave, let your best friend or partner read this chapter, and let them tell you! It's much easier to identify other people's scams than your own. Let's get really honest here, who wants to own up to having a scam? Only try this if you're feeling very brave, though, and have a very loving best friend or partner. NEVER, EVER show this chapter to anyone who could use it against you!

I won't kid you here, identifying your scam is not a pleasant process. It can be emotional when you begin to piece together the belief systems and unmet needs that you have been compensating for all your life. It can be terrifying too. These behaviours, our scams, serve us when we're not aware of what we're doing but as soon as you spot the scam, you have nowhere to hide.

However, no matter how horrific it is to discover what little scams you have been running in your life, it can also be a relief. It explains all sorts of weird behaviour that you might have indulged in and also helps you understand why you've done it. You will see clearly the benefits and pay-offs of your scams but usually we're only motivated to start busting our scam if the costs are out weighing the pay-offs. If this applies to you, try this three-step scambusting exercise, which will help you to find a healthier and more efficient way of getting what you need. Write your answers in your journal.

READY TO LEAP?
EXERCISE: SCAMBUSTING

Part 1: Identify your scam:

- What is your scam?
- When you're in full scam mode, what sort of things do you find yourself saying?
- When you're in full scam mode, what sort of things do you find yourself doing?
- Be very honest. What are the pay-offs for this behaviour?
- What is it costing you?
- Are you willing to give up your scam?

Part 2: What do you really need? (Identify your unmet needs)

If you're struggling to answer this question, ask yourself:

1 What do you really want? If I could wave a magical wand and give you three wishes that would mean you could create your ideal life, what would they be? (e.g. Lots of money? A loving partner? Your own private jet?)

2 Next, ask yourself what will these things get you? (e.g. Financial security? love and adoration? Freedom? Privacy?)

3 Finally, ask yourself what is it you really need to feel happy? What do you need to feel expanded, generous, at one with the world? Write your answers in your journal.

Part 3: Identify the belief system you are compensating for:

Identify the negative belief system at the root of your scam. Using the process we explored in Big Leap Step 3, create a new belief system that will support new, healthier, and more resourceful behaviours.

Then start to take some baby steps to create evidence to prove that this is true.

Make a Little Leap

Create and use three delicious daily habits. A daily routine will keep you focused, motivated and moving forward. Commit to doing three things each day that make your life healthier and happier. Pick things you want to do, not the ones that you think should. Make doing each your priority ,whether it's a candle-lit bath or dancing round the living room to your favourite music.

Baby Step 3: How to Bust your Scam

Our deepest fear is not that we are inadequate. Our deepest fear is that we are powerful beyond measure. It is our light, not our darkness, that most frightens us. We ask ourselves 'who am I to be brilliant, gorgeous, talented, fabulous?' Actually, who are you not to be?
Marianne Williamson

Busting your scams means taking a good look at the unmet needs and limiting beliefs that have held you back for so long and putting in place new beliefs and actions. It sounds easy, but this process really challenges your commitment to change. You want to change how you look at life, what you believe you can do and who you believe you can be and this is the way to make that a reality in your life. You may need to take a deep breath, but you know you can do it – it's just a matter of being vigilant and determined to succeed.

Busting the Cynic

The new belief: 'I can trust others.'

The scambuster: Instead of sneering cynically to protect yourself, try listening to what the other person is saying, perhaps do your own research and make an informed decision as to whether to trust the other person.

The baby step: You no longer automatically assume others are not to be trusted. You are willing to be open but you are still able to protect yourself by doing the research. You are building evidence that others/life can be trusted sometimes.

Busting the Martyr, the People-pleaser and the Rescuer

The new belief: 'I am loved for who I am, not for what I do for others. My needs are important.'

The Scambuster: Instead of doing things for others to get them to like you, start focusing on your own needs. Ask yourself 'What do I need here?'

The baby step: Ask friends and loved ones for what you need – whether it be for help, or a hug when you're feeling down. This will build the evidence that you don't have to do anything to be loved.

Busting the Joker

The new belief: 'I can just be me and people will like me and not attack me.'

The scambuster: Instead of immediately going into your well-known and full-blown comedy routine when you're in the company of others, start to share how you really think and feel about something – without adding a punch-line!

The baby step: If you're with people who know you very well, they may be waiting for the punch-line so perhaps only try out these new behaviours with new people or groups until you build your confidence and start to get accustomed to not being the joker.

Busting the Flake and the 'Blonde'

The new belief: 'I can shine and people won't attack me.'

The scambuster: Stop giggling, stop hiding your talents and start taking yourself seriously.

The baby step: Join a new social group where it would be appropriate for you to behave like the intelligent, incisive and likeable person you really are (try a book club or business networking group) and practice being your most brilliant self. Social convention will usually stop anyone from attacking you, which will give you space to let your brilliance shine in a safe environment.

Busting the Misery and the Drama Queen

The new belief: 'I am loved and listened to. I am heard.'

The scambuster: Talk to your friends and family about your unmet needs. Explain how important it is to be listened to and for your feelings to be heard and acknowledged. Coach them on how to listen to you and reflect back how you are feeling – ask them to listen without offering how to 'fix' you. When you start to believe that you don't have to have a problem or drama in order to command attention, the old behaviour will begin to fade.

The baby step: Set up a formal time to be 'listened to' weekly. Set ground rules – you must not be interrupted, there must be no judgements, you don't want to be fixed, you just want lots of hugs and acknowledgement at the end of your 'session'.

Busting the Rebel, the Vamp and the Stud

The new belief: 'I don't have to fight/seduce anyone to justify my place in the world, I can just be – and others will notice and love me.'

The scambuster: Instead of focusing on your impact on others, bring your attention to your own needs and wants. Figure out what you actually want to do with your time. What interests you, what do you do naturally, what do you enjoy doing?

The baby step: Create a 30-day Golden Glow project around what you love doing – as opposed to what you think will get you attention ...

Busting the Victim

The new belief: 'I am lovable.'

The scambuster: Take responsibility. As long as you are blaming others, and the world for your misfortunes, you will never be able to bust your scam.

The baby step: Be extremely compassionate with yourself and explore the idea that your beliefs about yourself create the reality you live in. If you change your beliefs, you can change your reality. Work with a therapist on healing childhood wounds and start to build evidence that you are lovable.

Busting the Adrenaline Addict

The new belief: 'I am good enough.'

The scambuster: Start cataloguing all the concrete evidence from your past that proves to you that you are good enough – from your qualifications to what your best friend has to say about you. Write it all down in your journal.

The baby step: When you feel the 'fear of failure', talk it through with a friend, instead of spiraling into your adrenaline-fuelled behaviour. Tune into your inner coach and listen to her advice.

Busting the Perfectionist and the Control Freak

The new belief: 'I am loved unconditionally.'

The scambuster: Learn to question your own set of internal rules about what is right and wrong. If you put your rules aside for a second, what do you really feel, want and need?

The baby step: Allow yourself to make minor errors/not create the perfect cakes/documents/artwork – and see that the world does not fall down around your ears. Notice you are likeable even though you're not perfect.

Get some therapy!

Because our scams can be compensations for certain needs that weren't met in childhood, sometimes it is useful to work with a therapist on healing any childhood wounds. A trained professional can create a compassionate space to vent your feelings and allow the healing process to begin. You may need therapy if:

- You can't think about your childhood without feeling angry, hurt or upset
- You cannot stop crying after reading the scam chapter.
- You feel you can never ever forgive the people who did this to you.
- You want to cut your parents out of your life forever.
- You have cut your parents out of your life forever and hate them with a boiling passion.

Make a Little Leap

Act weird! You've heard of thinking out of the box? Try acting out of the box. Today do everything the opposite of how you usually do it. Tell everyone that they're right, eat something that you say you can't stand, wear skin-tight pink leather trousers. Be aware how acting differently makes you and others feel. To create a different life, you have to 'do' differently – today make a start.

Baby Step 4: The Transition

Within us all there is both the sacred and profane, the sinner and saint, the dark and the light, and it is only by going through these secret passages, dark alleys and attics of our own mind that we can find the bliss of pure consciousness. Unless we embrace our own shadows, we are likely to be extremely judgemental of others and this moral self righteousness and need to judge causes turbulence with inner dialogues, which in turn causes us to lose connection with the spirit. Ceasing from judgement is part of silencing your internal dialogue.

Deepak Chopra

Scambusting cracks your shell and lets the 'real you' emerge. Yes, you can feel very vulnerable and 'naked' at first but it is also incredibly liberating. The real you is the one that isn't performing or making great efforts to get something. You just turn up and say what you have to say. You don't have to rehearse, you don't have to perform and you'll notice your behaviour begins to change. You become less poised, less tight and more relaxed and easy with yourself and others. You're in touch with what you really want and need and you can ask for it honestly rather than twisting yourself into a strange scam-like shape to get it. But there is a transition that you have to go through first. We have adopted our scam for a reason.

Bust your scam – and then what? Your fears of being unlovable, unsafe and unacceptable rush to the fore. 'Protect yourself, protect yourself!' screams your Inner Pessimist. You don't know who you are, you don't know how to react, you feel lost and scared of being rejected by others.

Not helped by the fact that other people may react negatively to the new you at first (after all, you've just changed the roles and the rules and they may not like it). 'What do you mean you're not going to rescue me/flirt with me/collude with my cynicism/smoke with me behind the shed anymore?' You may have to redefine your relationships. Be honest and tell them about your discoveries about yourself. Again, try not to point the finger and say: 'Well, if you weren't such a Misery, I wouldn't have to rescue you so much.' We don't know what is going on for other people. It's not up to us to bust anyone else's scam. Just stick with your own.

MAKING THE BIG LEAP:
Rachel Dobson, 30, Big Leaping from Sunday tabloid journalist to freelance journalist and property developer

I have never felt that I matched up to any of my friends or colleagues since I can remember. But I was always popular because I was a laugh. When I was a teenager I would drink the most, date gorgeous boys and always, always be up for a laugh. Booking a holiday? Dobbo will come. Having a party? Get Dobbo the icebreaker along.

Starting college I got along with everyone and anyone. I was never going to intimidate anyone – I was always the one to ask the stupid question, wear inappropriate clothes and do something for a joke. So I had friends, was comfortable, unchallenged and enjoyed myself.

Because I hid behind the mask of being a 'divvy' I never flourished. I never went for the job I really wanted – I never believed I would get it, after all I was the girl who made everyone else feel like Einstein, so how could I possibly work to that level? So the pay-off was that I paddled along in easy, junior positions, having a laugh, making friends, looking like I had a successful career. But the cost was that I wasn't proud of myself. I didn't feel I achieved anything. I was frustrated and unchallenged and resented people thinking I was less clever than I am. In fact, I have a first class honours degree – something only one other person on my course had achieved – but because it's not from Cambridge I took it off my CV. Any employer who's ever seen my CV thinks I landed my first job because of my secretarial qualifications – at least I didn't have to live up to anything.

Eventually, this started to gnaw away at me. I felt bitter and hated myself for not being brave enough to live up to what I thought I could become. People believed I really was a thicko because my work was terrible – I wasn't interested in it. I went through the motions at work: a cheery good morning every day and nobody guessed this role wasn't my life's ambition.

Working through the Big Leap exercises, it turned out my big need was for acclaim, which was quite a surprise to me. I was also looking for freedom to be myself, security to feel comfortable, lots of love and lots of fun too – that's still one of my key needs.

So I left my job and set up my own business – and I've never been so challenged in my whole life. I've had many, many moments when I've thought, who the hell do I think I am? What am I trying to do here? I spiral into meltdown and sob. Then I have to pick myself up and think: baby steps, baby steps. Thirty years of doing it one way (gulp – the waste!) has left its mark, but luckily that's not impossible to change. When I have a 'moment' I remind myself of past victories and dwell on them. I have a diary with five little things to do each day – ranging from sending an email to reading an article on something. I tick them off – happy at having done them, but not caring what the outcome of those actions is. But most of all I remember it's meant to be fun too. So I go out and have some fun – even if that just means roller-blading to the newsagents. Now I couldn't do that when I was stuck at work every day, could I?

The hard work was in identifying the scam. Once I did that, the work began and slowly, bit by bit, I started to recognize my old patterns of behaviour and started choosing a new way of being.

Ten ways you know you're in transition

- You suddenly don't know how to talk to your friends or partner.
- 'I don't know who I am any more' is your favourite phrase.
- You feel unsure about how to react in new situations – you don't have a comfortable 'routine' you fall into.
- If a crisis hits, you find yourself falling completely into your old scam and rescuing/flirting/snarling your way out of it.
- You find yourself at a loss when someone asks you 'what do you want to do tonight?'
- You question your motives about why you want to be around certain people – is it because you really like them or is it because you want to seduce, rescue or control them?
- You start having spectacular rows with friends, family and your partner.
- You don't go out as much.
- You find yourself bored and restless.
- Sometimes, you feel so sick with fear, you want to blot it all out and drink or take drugs, watch back-to-back films on the TV or sleep all day.

The no-judgement rule

Just as with our negative beliefs, our scams tend to hang around. In times of stress, my Martyr complex can quickly enter stage right huffing and puffing as she climbs the stairs. 'Okay . . .' she sighs. 'Who do you want me to help now?' I know how to operate with my scam in place. I feel protected. It gets me loved – albeit at a price. When working on our own self-development, we often feel that once we've 'seen' something about the way we operate then we're 'cured' so we believe that once our scam is busted then we'll lived happily ever after from that moment on. That's not been my experience. It's not 'getting rid' of the scam but rather being aware of it and then choosing to do something different in the moment. It's an on-going process.

That's why we have to put a no-judgement rule in place. When we see our scamming behaviour – either for the first time or ten years down the line, the easiest thing is to judge ourselves. When I first identified my Martyr scam, I had a field day. I felt I'd been behaving like a prostitute, I had been constantly pleasing other people for what they would 'pay' me in terms of affection and approval. I look back now and squirm at the extremes I went to with my Martyr scam. I practically put my whole career on hold for my husband so he could go and be successful (anything, anything, just please love me). I even promised a complete stranger a room to rent in my house because I sensed she didn't like me but I knew she needed somewhere to rent (I ended up taking her messages and doing her washing.) I once paid a £300 bar bill – the whole evening's drink bill for all our friends – because I'd got a little drunk, upset a friend and wanted to make sure she still liked me. Then I quietly and bitterly resented it.

When I looked back and counted the costs of my scam – both emotionally and financially – I wanted to weep and rage at myself. I judged myself for being stupid, pathetic: a prostitute for approval. But judging yourself, as I discovered, simply makes it worse. It makes you feel ashamed and utterly self-loathing, which doesn't help at all. In fact, it can simply be a new way to keep you obsessing about your inner dramas rather than getting on with the real task of creating a life that you adore. It's much easier to keep judging yourself because that keeps you stuck. You don't have to come out of your comfort zone and start to experiment with supportive and healthy new behaviours. Which admittedly can feel challenging, strange and scary.

You have to have the utmost compassion for yourself during the process of busting your scams and keeping them busted. After all, you were only doing what you thought was best at the time you created them. You weren't consciously playing these scams, and it's usually because you were too scared to do anything else that you created them so it takes courage and a lot of humility to identify then decide to do something about them. It can take moment-by-moment awareness sometimes but the more you are yourself, the easier life becomes.

Ten ways to know that your scam is busted

- You tell the truth.
- You no longer screen your telephone calls.
- Life becomes boring for about three months – and then peaceful.
- You spend time with people you adore and who adore you – and laugh a lot.
- You get absolutely clarity about what is the next step for you and you can't understand why you didn't see it before.
- Your days of procrastinating are over – you now get things done quickly and efficiently.
- You are kinder to others and to yourself.
- You stop trying to get your point across and listen more.
- You are happy to spend time alone.
- New friends come into your life, who you really like.

What your Inner Pessimist is probably saying now

'Don't get naked, your bum will frighten people. Are you insane? Drop your scam? How will you survive in the world without that? You'll be lost and miserable. No one will like you if you don't rescue/flirt/sneer/help. You know what? You're right. You are unlovable and unacceptable and you're right, you can't trust others. They'll just stab you in the back, you know they will. You don't know who you are and it's probably best it stays that way.'

READY TO LEAP?
EXERCISE: CALLING YOUR INNER COACH
Tune in to your Inner Coach. Write in your journal what your Inner Coach has to say about all this.

Take Ten Baby Steps

10 baby steps to take when you need to be strong but you just feel like crying.

1 Give up for an hour/day/week. Crawl under the duvet as often and as frequently as you can. Take time off, put in the bare minimum of energy and effort and surrender to how utterly low you feel.

2 Write down a list of your strengths – what are you naturally good at? Where do you excel? Now go and do one thing that allows you to show off your strength.

3 Cry – a lot. Cry until you can cry no more and your eyes are baggy. Sleep for a night, wake up and in the stillness of the morning, ask yourself: 'What is the next step I could take now?

4 Nourish yourself in every way possible – drink big pots of soup, wear big jumpers and socks, bring the duvet into the living room and wrap yourself in it and watch old films/ listen to your favourite comfort music/eat mashed potatoes.

5 Rant, moan, wail to your best friend. Inform them that they don't have to fix you, ask them just listen to you and nod. Get it all out of your system but set a time limit of two hours. Then write down ten things you are learning right now and ten things for which you are grateful.

6 If you were to cultivate 'inner strength' – what would the next piece of action you would take? Tell them to 'bog off', say nothing, have a quiet word?

7   Stand up, stand firm, plant your feet squarely, breathe into your belly and make that scary phone call. Then reward yourself in exaggerated and delightful ways.

8   Get others to be strong for you – gather your supporters, fans and friends and ask for help – be specific – give them instructions of exactly how they can support you to make the next step. E.g send your inspirational quotes/cook you dinner/help you write a business plan.

9   Make a decision that you're going to trust – trust yourself and trust that life is giving you exactly what you need to learn right now.

10   Switch off the phones, lock the door, close the blinds, speak to no one - hide away until you feel your strength return.

Big Leap Step 5:
Thunderbirds are go!

Just do it!

Take the first step in faith. You don't have to see the whole staircase, just take the first step.
   Dr Martin Luther King Jr

So, you've finally made it to the last step of the journey. Congratulations! Give yourself a gold star. You've done all the work beneath the surface, you've started to change and you feel different to the way you used to. Now it's time to go out into the external world and start making the changes to your life that will make your dreams come true. Get ready! It's time for ACTION! Yes, that means we actually have to DO something.

Big Leap Step 5: Taking the Baby Steps

1 Take one baby step, then another one...
2 The Gloop Zone
3 Meet the Saboteurs
4 Mind The Gap!
5 Tell us about the Money, Honey
6 450 baby steps – a 90-day plan
7 The F Word
8 The Big Leap – your homework

What you're probably thinking at Big Leap Step 5

- 'I can do this!'
- 'Just watch me everyone!'
- 'I'm so excited!'
- 'Bit nervous, but you know what? I think I can do this.'
- 'This is it!'
- 'Watch out world, here I come.'

What you're probably doing at Big Leap Step 5

- Putting new goals in your diary.
- Telling everyone to expect 'a few changes around here.'
- Throwing your fag packet out of the window/buying an exercise bike/signing up to recruitment agencies/resigning from your job.
- Throwing a party to signify your new life.
- De-cluttering your wardrobe/office/living room in preparation for your new life.
- Having your hair cut, buying new clothes.

Baby Step 1: Take one baby step, then another one...

A journey of a thousand miles must begin with a single step.
Lao Tsu

You've finally got to Big Leap Step 5, congratulations. Now it's time to prove the pudding is worth eating because this step requires you to start actually doing something. We've been working on the 'being' part, now you are required to do something and probably do it differently to how you've done it before. It's the old adage that the definition of madness is doing the same thing but expecting different results. So are you ready? Are your pencils sharpened, your shoes shiny, your new diary opened at a crisp new page? Are you ready to manifest the physical reality that has been created by your leap in thinking? This is the only time I'm going to say this but on this occasion, I don't want you to take a leap. I want you to take a baby step.

When we create exciting visions of our future, it can feel overwhelming and unrealistic at first and this is the danger point because we can simply dismiss the idea and go back into our comfort zones having done nothing. Even if we keep hearing the whispers of our Inner Coach calling we can simply turn up the TV so we can't hear her.

The first step is the scariest but it's the most significant. It shows you are willing to leave your comfort zone. But taking action can often be overwhelming. You don't know where to start. You look up at the mountain and the path to the top just looks too far and too long, suddenly you feel as if you'll never get to the top. That's why it's so important to take it one day at a time, cut everything into baby steps and keep taking the action. Those first few days and steps can be the scariest. Set yourself up to succeed and stop looking to the top of the mountain, keep looking down at the next step you're going to take. Repeat after me: 'I will achieve my goal with baby steps.'

By breaking our Big Leap down into baby steps, we creep out of our comfort zone without our fear claxons screaming: 'You're not good enough. You're going to fail.' I know we have talked about our Big Leap journey being based around our Golden Glow moments but fear can still sabotage us big style in the early days. We need to take it slowly and make our first steps small and manageable. After interviewing all my 'Big Leapers' for this book, they have suggested three first baby steps you could take, which they have found to be helpful.

First step: Get help

It's amazing who you know already who can make a difference to your success. Or if you don't know anyone, you'll probably know someone who does. You'll be surprised how much people actually like to help and share their knowledge. We all know how special and wanted it can make us feel if someone approaches us as an 'expert'. I always feel incredibly flattered when someone wants to pick my brains. So who do you know that can help you?

Make a list of potential mentors, enthusiastic friends, friends of parents and old bosses who can help you work towards your goal then create a blanket email to send to everyone and ask for help. But be specific: state what your goal is and ask for help giving examples – e.g. does anyone's company do so and so? Does anyone know anyone in New York that I can stay with?

Second step: Get support

Form a Big Leap support group. Get your two best and most positive friends on board and form your group. Tell them your plans and ask them to be there for you and to tell you, 'you can do it', 'you're amazing', 'of course, you can run for president' whenever you're having a crisis of confidence. It is so important to create a support team of friends or colleagues – a 'power team' – who can hold your hand when you feel tired and emotional and who will applaud your triumphs. Make sure you avoid negative pessimists like the plague.

MAKING THE BIG LEAP:
Nicky Hambleton Jones, 32, Big Leaping from management consultant to celebrity fashion stylist and business owner

People think you need contacts to start a business or be successful – it's that 'it's who you know, not what you know' line. That's rubbish. I didn't know a single soul in fashion but still managed to create a business in the fashion industry. It's not contacts that you need, it's your support team – your coach, your friends, those people who believe in you 110 per cent. They are the ones, who will tell you to keep the faith, in your darkest hour and who'll push you to keep going when you doubt yourself.

Third step: Find your tribe

It can be very difficult to create the life you want if you are surrounded by people who think you're slightly odd for even trying. They can make you feel like you're either insane or headed for a mighty fall. Instead you need to surround yourself with like-minded people, people who are also creating their dreams. Seek them out: for support, for laughs and for inspiration. On my Big Leap journey, I have often been inspired by others – sometimes just at the right time. My business was turned around by going to a presentation and hearing Simon Woodruffe (the business entrepreneur who created Yo-Sushi!) challenging everyone in the audience to do tomorrow what each of us had put off for months. The next day, I sent an email that got me a column in the national press. I may never have sent that email if I hadn't been with people who had been there themselves and got the tee-shirt.

In everyone's life, at some time, our inner fire goes out. It is then burst into flame by an encounter with another human being. We should all be thankful for those people who rekindle the inner spirit.
   Albert Schweitzer

MAKING THE BIG LEAP:
Donal Doherty, 28, Big Leaping from bar manager to Director of Egoscue Method in London

Find your tribe! Too right! It is so important to surround yourself with people, who encourage you and are on similar journeys. When I shared my plans with friends from the bar they thought I was insane. Well-meant but poorly directed scepticism is not great for your confidence. I had to make the leap from being a bar manager to being an Egoscue therapist and businessman and so I wanted to surround myself with like-minded people. I soon made a new set of friends, who didn't sneer when I told them my plans for global domination! It takes effort but it pays off. You don't constantly feel that you've arrived at a black-tie do wearing fancy dress. Making the leap is a challenge. By having the right people around you it becomes easier, and a lot more fun!'

Baby Step 2: The Gloop Zone

There is no problem so big it can't be run away from.
Charles Schultz

Go on then. What are you waiting for? You've written your lists of baby steps, you've got your friends screaming support on the sideline, you've joined an entrepreneurial networking group for support. Now what? What do you mean 'Nothing'?

Welcome to the Gloop Zone. The Gloop Zone is that terrifying void of non-action when 'something gets in the way' of you taking the first step: the baby's up all night, the boss decided they wanted an early morning meeting, your partner is having a crisis and needs your help and all of a sudden your good intentions fly out of the window.

Another day passes where you've done nothing to build evidence to prove that your new life is possible and then another and you sink further and further into the Gloop. You feel your passionate fervour ebbing away until you find yourself at the end of the week in the same chair, watching the same TV programme, thinking 'Noooooooooooooooo!'

The Inner Pessimist loves the Gloop Zone. 'Ah, you see, I told you you couldn't do it.' It feeds off your inertia. 'Well, you've tried, never mind, well done for reading that book but it's time you came back to reality.'

The Gloop Zone is where I usually turn into a cynic. It's where I blame the process: 'That book? Oh, yeah, I read it too but it just doesn't work.' The Gloop Zone is where my best intentions are knobbled. It's the place where I threw my fag packet out of the window, bought an exercise bike and signed up to the newest yoga class – and then did nothing. The Gloop Zone is the place I've read books like this and fished dog ends of cigarettes out of the bin to smoke, watched dust gathering on the exercise bike, been so hung-over I'd have to put down the book and have a lie down, while at the same time promising that my new 'regime' will start tomorrow.

Ten ways you'll know that you're in the Gloop Zone

- You say things like 'I'll start this tomorrow.'
- You find yourself avoiding looking in your diary.
- You get angry with your friends or family saying: 'Don't give me a hard time', if they mention that they thought you were doing that new thing . . .
- You find yourself doing displacement activities like shopping/drinking in the pub/watching TV.
- You find yourself getting involved in other people's dramas.
- You feel lethargic.
- Your home either becomes a tip as you sit around and pick your toe-nails or it becomes a palace as you clean every surface for the fifth time: 'I'll just get sorted out before I start.'
- You are drinking 14 cups of tea a day.
- You eat non-stop.
- You find yourself volunteering for other people's errands. 'I'll pick up your dry cleaning for you.'

In some ways being in the Gloop Zone is even worse than being in denial in Big Leap Step 1, because now it's conscious. You know why you've been unhappy, you know what little scams you've had running and you still find yourself sitting in the same chair. The Gloop Zone becomes a pit of despair and self-loathing as your Inner Pessimist sits beside you, gloating and patronizing you: 'It's okay, dear, you've done ever so well but a fulfilled life? Not for you, really, is it?'

How long we stay in the Gloop Zone is usually in direct relation to how scared we are about making our Big Leap. Staying in the Gloop Zone is just another way to keep ourselves safe. At this point we have to be very, very kind to ourselves. You've probably been here a million times before and how has beating ourselves up about it ever helped? Your Inner Pessimist is so terrified right now that he'd sell your grandma to keep you where you are.

Try this exercise. Go to bed, get under the duvet and acknowledge you're in the Gloop Zone. Then get your journal and do the following exercises:

- What are you scared might happen if you take a baby step?
- What's the absolute worst case scenario?
- How would you handle that?
- What is the tiniest baby step you can make today?
- How can you could make that tinier?
- What do you commit to do when you get out of bed?

Baby Step 3: Meet the Saboteurs

You must do the thing you think you cannot do.
  Eleanor Roosevelt

So you're out of the Gloop, you're taking your baby steps and you're slowly creeping your way out of your comfort zone. Or perhaps you're storming ahead, you've written your resignation letter, you've got your meetings planned, you're about to head off to the sun to look at some properties and you're all set to go. Your Inner Pessimist seems fairly quiet, but then you start to notice some other weird noises and behaviours.

I'd like you to meet the Saboteurs, the second cousin of the Inner Pessimist. Your Saboteurs tend to gang together on the street corner of your inner fears. Effectively, they gather around you looking threatening, stopping you from moving forward. They are very familiar, old behaviours that you have in place to slow you down or to sabotage your success. Just as with the Inner Pessimist, it's no good doing battle with them. You created them unconsciously because you were terrified – of success, of failure, of not being good enough, whatever it was. So don't try to ignore them or bully them into submission, it won't work. You have to be gentle with yourself and them. Bring them into the light of awareness and discover the next layer of fear that stops you from moving forward.

Procrastination is my favourite Saboteur. In fact, I'd say that procrastination is one of my greatest skills. I've become such a master at procrastination and it has become so subtle that I can fool myself into thinking that I'm not procrastinating at all but in the middle of the 'creative process' or 'doing research' or 'getting in touch with my feelings', when in fact, I'm out shopping and drinking wine with my best friend.

I'm good at creating the big vision, talking-the-talk, describing how my life will look in five years time, getting everyone excited and busting my scams. And this can go on for days, months and sometimes even years. I dream, I plan, I visualize – but I do nothing. My husband – an immensely practical man – always raises an eyebrow when I get out my coloured pens and draw circles around ideas and write up a little schedule of when I'm going to get it done (always starting tomorrow, of course).

Tomorrow is a lovely place to park your dreams because if you plan your procrastination well, tomorrow never comes. 'Tomorrow' you don't have to be disappointed when 'he' doesn't turn up, devastated when 'they' say no, when the banks laugh, when you fail so spectacularly that even your biggest fans start to doubt you. Procrastination allows you to live in 'I-could've-been-a-contender-land' and sometimes that feels a great deal pleasanter than the imagined sound of mocking laughter. I know exactly why I procrastinate and sometimes I let myself settle there comfortably for a day or two while I gather my courage and prepare to throw myself out of my comfort zone again.

As human beings, we're not stupid. Our Saboteurs are there to protect us, to try to keep us safe in our comfort zone. However, to live the life you really want, we're going to venture out of your comfort zone and make the Big Leap. And part of that leap means bringing our Saboteurs into awareness. I have detailed the seven main saboteurs below. Once you have read them all, complete the exercise that follows and write your procrastinating symptoms on a big sheet of paper so no matter how wily you may be, you will never be able to convince yourself that shopping and drinking white wine with your best friend is research.

SABOTEUR NUMBER 1: THE PROCRASTINATOR

Saboteur style: Shifty

Most likely to say: 'I'll just clean the house – from top to bottom – before I start doing it.'

You know you're sabotaging when:

- You spend every day rewriting your vision.
- You spend all your time telling everyone what your new life will look like but do nothing different.
- Your house/office/desk is always scrupulously tidy – once everything is tidy, you'll start working on the baby steps 'tomorrow'.
- You decide to start taking action once you've stopped smoking/in a -better position/got married/moved house/lost weight.
- You don't make the phone call because everyone's away for Christmas or the summer or because the kids are on holiday.
- You don't make the call because they might be on their mobile or they might be in a meeting.
- You have spent the whole day on the Internet 'researching' and once you have a bit more information, you'll make the call.

Why you do it? It's easier to put off living your dreams than facing possible disappointments, heartbreaks and failure. By procrastinating, you live the fantasy but you are not actually moving forward.

SABOTEUR NUMBER 2: THE OVER-PROMISER

Sabotage style: Effusive, big arm movements, large figures bandied about.

Most Likely to say: 'By this time next year, we'll be millionaires.'

You know you're sabotaging when:

- You talk and your friends' eyes glaze over.
- You talk and the bank manager says: 'Er, are we both looking at the same account?'
- You consistently set goals that you never reach.
- Your credit card is declined – often.
- Even you don't believe your hype.
- You spend more time shopping for the accessories to go with the lifestyle you're going to have, than getting on with doing what needs to be done to get the lifestyle in the first place.

Why you do it? By living in 'bigg-ed up world', you don't have to face the nitty-gritty of putting in the hours to get what you want and you don't have to confront your fears by facing reality.

SABOTEUR NUMBER 3: THE FLAKE

Sabotage style: Flaky.

Most likely to say: 'Oops, I left the baby on the bus.'

You know you're sabotaging when:

- You show up late to important meetings.
- You miss trains.
- You 'don't hear the alarm.'
- You lose the keys to the car.
- You lock yourself out of the car/the house/the office.
- You can't find the very important business card/file.

Why you do it? Playing flaky means you don't have to take responsibility for your plans not coming to fruition. You can blame failure on everyone and everything else – the late train or the alarm.

SABOTEUR NUMBER 4: THE WILD CHILD

Sabotage style: Hunched

Most likely to say: 'I don't give a s**t what you think.'

You know you're sabotaging when:

- You're rude to important people.
- You have too much to drink and behave inappropriately at a business social occasion.
- You drink too much/take drugs the night before a big day.
- You turn up to important meetings in inappropriate clothes.

Why you do it? You're terrified that someone will attack you or tell you your idea can't work so you hunch into a defensive stance and hope that they'll be too scared to try.

SABOTEUR NUMBER 5: THE PERFECTIONIST

Sabotage style: Scary, bossy and controlling.

Most likely to say: 'Rewrite it.'

You know you're sabotaging when:

- You re-write something seven times and it's still not right.
- You refuse to send it out until it's perfect.
- You fixate on one route and insist that this is the only way.

- You tell everyone how to do his or her job.
- You tell everyone that they're wrong and you're right.
- Your voice gets more and more clipped.
- You start criticizing others for not getting small details right.

Why you do it? Terror of moving forward. If it's not perfect, you know it won't work. So why risk rejection and failure just yet?

SABOTEUR NUMBER 6: THE BEACH BUM

Sabotage style: Horizontal.

Most likely to say: 'Don't get your knickers in a twist, I'm doing it in my own time.'

You know you're sabotaging when:

- You light 'just one more' joint/have 'just one more' beer.
- You smile charmingly and shrug when anyone asks you a specific question about your plans.
- You sit around with other people who are also being sabotaged by the beach bum behaviour and 'just chill'.
- You buy a skateboard or scooter to help you get creative.

Why you do it? You're completely terrified of committing to something because deep down you don't think you have the resources to make it happen – so you 'chill' instead.

SABOTEUR NUMBER 7: THE FEELER

Sabotage style: Anxious

Most likely to say: 'Let's talk about how I'm feeling.'

You know when you're sabotaging when:

- You fantasize about how your life will be when you're 'discovered' but you do nothing.
- You write your Oscar speech rather than rewrite your CV.
- You want everything to be 'beautiful' but because it isn't, you do nothing.
- You sit at home writing in your journal about your feelings.
- You talk endlessly about your feelings to your friends.
- You enviously obsess about what other people have or what they're doing with their lives.
- You live in a fantasy-land in the future and resist anything that feels remotely 'ordinary'.

Why you do it? You are terrified that you can't create the life you want, but also fear that the reality will never live up to the fantasy.

READY TO LEAP?
EXERCISE: IDENTIFY YOUR SABOTEURS
Answer the following questions in your journal:

- What are your usual Saboteurs?
- What is your particular sabotage style?
- What do you usually say when in sabotage mode?
- Describe in great detail the series of events or actions you take or don't take when you're sabotaging yourself?
- What are your top three sabotaging symptoms? (Shopping? Skateboarding? Talking about your feelings?)

Make a Little Leap
Be brave! Take a leap rather than a baby step today and do something that's a stretch for you – from asking a stranger on a date to asking your boss for a raise. The more we get used to stepping out of our comfort zones, the easier changing our habits will be and reaching our goals will be.

The Saboteur antidote

So what's the answer to the saboteur? Awareness is the key. Awareness and baby steps. Once you know how you sabotage yourself and can catch yourself in the process, you're half way there. You then simply have to acknowledge that you're scared, but as the uber-guru Susan Jeffers says: 'feel the fear and do it anyway'.

Make it as painless and unscary as possible by taking a baby step. As soon as you take a small step towards your goal, the fear recedes, which results in you able to move forward again. I call it exercising the courage muscle. The more you exercise this muscle, the stronger it gets and before you know it, you're taking massive leaps without a saboteur lurking on the horizon.

> **Saboteur antidote**
>
> - Awareness + baby step = little leap.
> - Little leap + little leap + little leap =
>   strong courage muscles =
>   Big Leap.

MAKING THE BIG LEAP:
Nicky Hambleton Jones, 32, Big Leaping from management consultant to celebrity fashion stylist and business owner

I had my business idea, had the business plan, had been on the styling course and I think I could have spent a year procrastinating designing logos, letterheads and web sites before getting my first client. But my coach bullied me – she calls it motivation! – into styling my first ever client and taking her out on a shopping trip. I nearly died of nerves – but I did it. The results were fantastic. My client loved it and felt completely transformed. A week later she flew off on a holiday and met the love of her life. It really boosted my confidence.

I think it's a common mistake to make when you start your new business. You spend ages concentrating on the details rather than on the brass tacks. If I didn't have any clients, I wouldn't have a business. That first client will always be terrifying, but whatever you have to do to get through the fear – just do it.

Baby Step 4: Mind The Gap!

Getting ahead in a difficult profession – singing, acting, writing, whatever – requires avid faith in yourself. You must be able to sustain yourself against staggering blows and unfair reversals. When I think back to those first couple of years in Rome, those endless rejections, without a glimmer of encouragement from anyone, all those failed screen tests, and yet I never let my desire slide away from me, my belief in myself and what I felt I could achieve.

   Sophia Loren

You've made your way out of the Gloop, you've found your Saboteur antidote but I'm afraid to say there may be times when you still feel as if you're going insane. You have the vision in place, you have printed out your business cards, you have big plans afoot for global domination but you're in debt, you're still working out of your back bedroom and you're still working full-time in a job you don't like.

The gap between how you envisioned your new life would be and the reality of how it is right now can sometimes seem too ludicrously wide. You wonder whether you're simply a fantasist who makes things up so they feel better. Your Inner Pessimist sniggers knowingly as you open a bank statement and you feel your heart drop.

So how do you survive these moments when your Inner Pessimist urges you to turn back, reassuring you that you made a good effort, but telling you it's time to go back to reality now. How do you keep going when all the signs tell you to turn back and 'be realistic'.

MAKING THE BIG LEAP:
Donal Doherty, 28, Big Leaping from bar manager to Director of Egoscue Method in London

I sat on the sofa with a lap full of unpaid bills – the phone bill, the credit card bills, even the rent was due and I thought 'Why am I doing? Is everyone right? Am I really that stupid and foolish?' I have to admit that I did freak out. Metaphorically, I hid underneath the bed for a few days and didn't answer the door. Until I heard a little voice asking: 'In a hundred years, who's going to give a damn? People go out on a limb all the time and many only achieve success after a number of attempts.' I thought: 'If this doesn't work, there's always another way.' I stopped taking it all so seriously. No one was going to die. As soon as I lightened up, life opened up once more, I got my first clients and opportunities just began to appear. It began slowly at first and the tempo kept increasing. Fear just seizes you up. And I'm sure people can smell it. My advice? Don't do anything when you're hiding under the bed. Do whatever it takes to relax and then things will start happening for you.

Is there anything you can do to help you get from out from under the bed? At points like this in the journey, it's useful to check in with yourself. If the journey is becoming too much of a struggle it's usually because your belief is wavering and an emotional need is not being met. To get back on track, go back to some of big leap basics before you start taking baby steps.

READY TO LEAP?
EXERCISE: BIG LEAP CHECK-LIST
Answer the following questions in your journal:

1 **Needy?**

   What emotional need is not being met right now? What do I need that I'm not getting? How can I get that need met?

2 **Tuned in to the wrong station?**

   Who am I listening to, my Inner Pessimist or my Inner Coach? Meditate for 15 minutes and then write down what your Inner Coach has to say.

3 **Bingo moment?**

   Does my vision excite me and make feel inspired and uplifted even if I don't know how on earth I'm going to create it?

4 **Belief?**

   What am I assuming right now that is blocking me? What do I need to believe about myself and life to enable me to make the next step?

5 **Scams?**

   What old behaviours are showing up right now that might be slowing me down? What is at the root of that?

6 **Saboteurs?**

   How am I sabotaging myself right now? What tiny baby step can I take in the next 10 minutes?

Baby Step 5: Tell us about the Money, Honey

I don't know much about being a millionaire, but I'll bet I'd be a darling at it.
  Dorothy Parker

Lack of money is often the problem that brings most Big Leaps to a grinding halt. Money is linked not only to our emotional needs for security but also to our survival needs. All the meditating and visualizing in the world won't pay the bills or put food on the table. When we are constantly focusing on our vanishing bank accounts, it feels impossible, painful and terrifying to even think about making the Big Leap.

I wish I'd known all this when I made my Big Leap. I must admit that I'm rather an optimist. I had finished my training to be a Life Coach, spent a small fortune on my letterhead, bought a headset for my phone and then sat like a lemon and waited for it to ring. And of course it didn't. The bills began to flood in, my debts began to stack up, as did my anxiety levels. Three months in and I was panicking: 'But this is my dream job. I've had my bingo moment. Why isn't it working?' I felt twitchy, envious of others. I felt closed down, strained, desperate. I would have coached anyone with a pulse. No one volunteered.

Are you surprised? Donal was right with his comments earlier. People can smell fear and desperation. When you have unmet survival needs, you are going nowhere fast. It becomes a downward spiral. Remember, what you focus on expands, so the more you focus on the lack, the more lack you attract, which means you focus on it even more. It's a vicious cycle.

My husband started huffing and puffing in the background as the debts began to seep through to the joint account. 'Don't you believe in me?' I screamed. 'Do you believe in yourself?' asked my coach. If our belief systems create our reality, what belief was creating this current reality? When I explored this with my coach, it was my 'not good enough' stuff floating to the surface again. I had just qualified as a coach, how did I know I was good enough? What evidence did I have? Not a lot.

I needed to build my belief systems and really 'know' that I was a good coach, I also had to build my business and profile so that people would know how to get hold of me. This process takes time. I needed to find part-time work in the meantime so that I wasn't reliant on my coaching work to support me financially.

As Big Leaper Nicky advises (below), it can take more time that we estimate to create the life we want. If we want to enjoy the journey, we need to take the pressure off ourselves as we build the evidence to support our new belief systems and build our new lives.

The words that strike dread into my heart is when a client, inspired and full of enthusiasm after completing their vision and wild-eyed from their Bingo moment, tells me that they have resigned from their job that morning. With no money coming in, that enthusiasm and inspiration will drain away as quickly as water draining from a bath.

You need to be able to support yourself financially on your Big Leap journey if you want to have a pleasant ride. This may mean you have to stay in your full-time job and retrain during the evening and at weekends, just as Big Leaper Salma Shah is doing, but at least you'll be financially secure. Take a leaf out of Salma's book: she won't be leaving her job in IT until she has a full coaching practice or a corporate coaching contract in the bag.

When Nicky was made redundant she rented out her house while she stayed with friends and built up her business. Even though Andrew took the Big Leap and travelled to Hong Kong without many savings, he had his own flat in London and so he knew that if things got really bad, he could always sell that.

Yes, it takes a leap of faith to make the Big Leap but it's a lot less scary if you create a safety net, so don't shy away from the financial or practical issues of working out exactly how are you going to do this?

Answer these questions about the financial side of your big leap in your journal before you do anything drastic.

READY TO LEAP?
EXERCISE: MONEY-MAKING LEAPS

- How much money do you need to make your Big Leap?
- How do you intend to finance your Big Leap?

- What will you have to believe about yourself to finance this Big Leap?
- How could you possibly use money to sabotage your Big Leap?
- What does your Inner Coach have to say about the money?
- What five baby steps could you can make this week to create a sound financial plan?
- What practical steps can you take that will start putting this plan into action? For example, could you discover a way to moonlight in order to save £100 a week for the next 3 months, investigate part-time jobs or get a student or career loan?

MAKING THE BIG LEAP:
Nicky Hambleton Jones, 32, Big Leaping from management consultant to celebrity fashion stylist and business owner

Set yourself up to succeed by overestimating the time it will take. If you think it'll take one month to set up a bank loan, allow four months. If you think it will take two months to set up a business alliance, allow six months. Everything takes much longer that you think it will. Sometimes I felt like giving up because I'd have days and days without one phone call. Then something amazing would happen – like an article would be published in a newspaper and I'd be inundated. But you can't rely on a new business for all your income. It took me two years before I could start earning a decent wage. My turnover for the first year was £3000! At one point, I rented out my flat and was living in friends' houses to save money. I also had to get a part-time job. That was my saviour. Most businesses fail because of cash flow in the early days so make sure you have some other source of income. It's also very isolating when you start your own business so a part-time job is great just for company.

Make a Little Leap

Get more than you need in every area of you life. What do you need more of in your life? Time, space, money, energy, love? Figure out what you need to be happy and healthy, then double it. Then plan a way of getting it – whether that be sitting down your loved ones and asking for support or scheduling in three nights a week where you do nothing but lie in bed and sleep. You can reach your goals by changing even the small things. For example, need more money to reach your goals? Look at your daily habits. Your morning slug of double latte costs you £1.60 a day, that's £416 a year you could save if you got to like the taste of instant coffee or even better gave up coffee altogether. To inspire you further, if you invested that at 10 per cent, you'd have £23,826 savings over 20 years! Glass of water anyone?

Baby Step 6: 450 baby steps – a 90-day plan

There is a vitality, a life force, an energy, a quickening that is translated through you into action, and because there is only one of you in all of time, this expression is unique. And if you block it, it will never exist through any other medium and it will be lost. The world will not have it. It is not your business to determine how good it is nor how valuable nor how it compares with other expressions. It is your business to keep it yours clearly and directly, to keep the channel open.
    Martha Graham

Once you've got the money flowing again, I want you to keep moving, I don't want you to stop. Create a 90-day plan by taking five baby steps a day and 25 baby steps a week. Create a special notebook and write a list of five baby steps for every day for the first week (but not for the whole 90 days as things tend to change and speed up as the month goes on). Your baby steps can be small – such as phone call to a business development agency or a call to book a meeting with a web site designer. The main objective is to plant your seeds. Every baby step that you take is another seed planted.

Set yourself up to succeed by celebrating at the end of every week. Ring your support group and get them to cheer loudly. Don't wait until you've climbed your mountain before you throw the party: celebrate every molehill you leap over. It helps give you momentum.

At the end of 30 days, reflect, congratulate yourself and then plan the next 30 days. What has worked? What hasn't worked? Use the foundation and confidence you have built up over the last 30 days to create a springboard for next seed-planting mission. Remember: if you keep on doing what you've always done, you'll keep on getting what you've always got. The main focus is to keep taking the actions and to keep planting your seeds. As with seeds, they can take a while to grow but by the end of your 90-day programme, you might see the first few shoots of life. It is incredible how fast a garden can grow, if the ground is fertile. You've done all the hard work so there is no reason why your garden should not be growing at an alarming rate.

Baby Step 7: The F Word

For me, failure is not about things not turning out as I wanted them. For me failure is when I don't attempt the things which in my heart I know I want to.
  Anon

But what if it doesn't? What if your garden doesn't grow? What if your garden looks like it isn't blooming and you can only see a few weeds beginning to sprout? If you're normal, you will probably be hit so hard and be so paralyzed by the fear of failure that you hide away – maybe for weeks, maybe forever.

When you're on the Big Leap journey, fear of failure is a biggie. It is the one fear that the Inner Pessimist doesn't have to shout. One little whisper is enough to stop us dead in our tracks. Our Big Leap journey is about aligning our whole lives with our passions, fulfilling our purpose – so where do you go from here if you fail spectacularly? Wouldn't it be terrible to get this far and discover your Inner Pessimist is right? You feel such a fool to have tried. But it's about more than fear of feeling foolish. It would be like witnessing the death of your dreams.

Failure. Most of us have been burnt by it or branded by it whether it was as a child, teenager or adult. And it's hideous. So when my coach told me that there was no such thing as failure but simply a 'learning experience', I had to disagree. No such thing as failure? Fear of failing had kept me up too many nights to let this one pass without a fight.

How would our worlds be different if we weren't scared of failure, she asked? How would life be different if failure was seen as one of the best things we could do in life? How would life be different if failure was honoured and we gave awards for it – Great Failures of the Year – that we took pride in listing our failures? What would it be like if failure wasn't a full stop but the base point for leaping to a whole new level? How would our lives be different if we brought up our children with a healthy respect for failure because failure was linked to our greatest learning experiences? What if there was no such thing as failure, just simply a learning experience?

Big Leaper Nicky Hambleton Jones first hired me because she felt she was 'failing'. At 30, she was washed up. All her friends were working in great careers, were successful and she had just been made redundant for the third time as a management consultant. 'It's official,' she wailed. 'I'm a failure.' What if there was no such thing as failure and this was the best learning experience of your life – what are you learning? 'That I've been in the wrong, bloody job for ten years!' she snapped back. So what is the right job?

That question started Nicky off on a path upon which she identified that she hated working for other people, that she wasn't in the least bit inspired or interested by management consultancy and in fact, she wanted to start, and run, her own fashion business. Three years on, Nicky has her own fashion company, make-up range and TV show. 'Without "failing" in corporate life, I would never have discovered my dream and wouldn't be here now. Failing was the best thing I've ever done', she says now. 'It was my wake-up call to life.'

Imagine if every failure was a wake-up call to life? How would this magical thinking serve you? What if failure was seen as a profoundly positive experience? That it allowed us to re-evaluate our lives and our path, and ask ourselves the questions that we probably choose to ignore in less turbulent times: What do we REALLY want? What are we good at? What are we TRULY interested in?

Okay, so let's say the initial feeling of 'failing' doesn't feel good. We're disappointed that things didn't work out as we hoped they would and it can be annoying and irritating – but aren't all wake-up calls? When I'm woken from a deep sleep, I certainly feel grumpy, annoyed and irritated. We may be irritated but at least we're alive, breathing and 'awake'. We're not living a life of 'quiet desperation', plodding along on the same, old non-challenging path for years because we're scared of doing something different.

Without that wake-up call, we live with an enemy that is far greater than failure. Failure is not our greatest enemy. It's fear of failure than can truly do us in. What has your fear of failure stopped you from doing? From finding the love your life? From creating a global company? From writing a best-seller? Maybe we were saved from feeling foolish, but at what cost? Our fear of failure just holds us back, stops us from trying and from truly living. Maybe we could have been a contender, but in the end we were too scared.

Back in the 1950s, in America, one of the best ways that struggling new talent could start on the road to fame and fortune was to appear on a nationally televised programme called the Ted Mack Amateur Hour. A singer from Tennessee tried out for the show, but failed the audition. The Oxford English Dictionary defines 'failed' as unsuccessful, not good enough, weak or deficient. Imagine if that singer had defined himself a failure, unsuccessful, not good enough. The world would never have known Elvis Presley.

Whether it's Elvis, Margaret Mitchell with her 25 rejections for *Gone with The Wind*, or Thomas Edison's efforts with the light bulb, what would have happened if they had been so afraid of making a fool of themselves and of being further disappointed that they gave up and gave in?

But how DO we make the magical shift from 'I'm a failure, I'm doomed, I'll never amount to anything' to 'there's no such thing as failure, just a learning experience'. If you have a belief that you're not good enough, failure is absolutely invaluable as evidence to prove that it's true. In fact, we may constantly, albeit subconsciously, set ourselves up to fail, so we can prove to ourselves that this belief is true. If this resonates with you, it may be useful to go back and re-read Step 3. Remember, beliefs are simply a filter through which we see the world and through which we will filter all our experiences to make sure they back up our essential beliefs about ourselves and life.

Our way into a new magical way of thinking, of 'learning' rather than 'failing', is built on a foundation of self-belief. Belief that if something does not turn out as we hoped, it doesn't mean that there's something wrong with us. It's about being able to let go of the idea of perfection, of 'getting it right first time', of having a bar 'this high' we have to jump over to prove that we're okay. What if you just knew that you were okay – no matter what the result of what you were trying to achieve in life? If our self-belief and self-esteem is all wrapped up in what we 'do', then it is easy to see why failure is so painful.

When you hear the whispers of the fear of failure, try this exercise. Answer the following questions in your journal:

READY TO LEAP?
EXERCISE: WHAT ARE YOU LEARNING?

- How are things not turning out as you hoped?
- What would happen if you let go of the outcome?
- How could these results be a call to action?
- What Big Leap in thinking do you need to take?
- If you were to look back at this 'crisis' in ten years time, what do you think you will have learnt here?
- If this were to be the moment where you completely re-invented your idea/business/thinking, what three pieces of action would you take/or not take?

Sometimes it's useful to take some 'under the duvet' time, as I call it. Time when we stop pushing, stop checking our emails to discover if 'they've' replied and simply take time out and let life get on with it. It goes against every notion that we have in Western society but sometimes 'giving in' and surrendering so we can take time out is exactly what we need to do. Sometimes when we push really hard and get overly intent on a particular outcome, we don't realize that life has other plans. We're so close to the process that we can't see the grand plan. Our Inner Pessimist gets more and more panicked by the lack of results, giving him more and more ammunition to throw at us and so when he finally throws the 'failure' grenade into our laps, we explode.

But sometimes, we need an explosion – to explode our beliefs, our expectations and our plans. In the aftermath of the explosion, we're so exhausted and shocked that we can finally find some peace so we can hear what our Inner Coach has been telling us all along. Usually she'll tell us there's no such thing as failure and asking if we had thought of doing it this way instead? And our journey begins afresh once again. We realize that they weren't weeds growing in our garden but simply new, different ideas that we simply didn't recognize as such because we'd planted something else.

Baby Step 8: The Big Leap – your homework

The question is not whether we will die, but how we will live.
Joan Borysenko

Your garden will start to bloom at some stage – maybe not exactly as you thought – but bloom it will. It may take longer than 90 days, maybe a year, even two or three but there will come a point where you no longer have to drive the changes: the company starts to make money; watching the sun come up over Hong Kong harbour is a regular occurrence rather than an occasional one; you've created your web site and the orders are flooding in.

This doesn't mean you can sit back and put your journal away. I'm afraid I'm going to give you some homework. This is an ongoing journey. As we've discussed before, it's not about getting 'there'. You're 'there' now. You create your life in this moment, you plant the seed now. No waiting is allowed. Your Big Leap is just one thought away. That's why it helps to keep your journal up to date and with you at all times: writing it is an excellent way to coach yourself to keep on making your leaps. It's a great way to keep in touch with your Inner Coach and also a good place for your Inner Pessimist to have a good old rant in a place where you can keep an eye on him.

So don't put your journal away. Let it be your wand of transformation. Let it be the safe place where you bring your demons, saboteurs and pessimist into the light of awareness so they no longer lurk in the dark and destroy your dreams. The more aware we become of the fears that block you, the more will look be able to make true choices about where you want to direct your lifs. Let your journal be the place where you re-connect with your Inner Coach, where her voice gets strong and clear, where you are able to recognize her wisdom and take actions from a new place of knowing. Let it be the place where you truly celebrate your success – where you learn to cheer yourself on, to be kind to yourself, to give yourself the positive, affirming messages that you've maybe always longed to hear but never could over the ranting of your inner pessimist. Let your journal be a book of hope when all the lights seems dim, let it be your inspiration, your manual to guide you to your new life – your own personal guidebook for your new way of working, living and being.

WHAT YOUR INNER COACH IS SAYING RIGHT NOW
Smile. Relax. Enjoy.

Take Ten Baby Steps

10 baby steps to take when you're exhausted but have a mountain to climb

1   Before you go to sleep write the question to the answer that you think would solve the problem that is exhausting you and wait for inspiration in your dreams.

2   Ask yourself – what unmet need is driving me to feel so exhausted and how can I get that need met?

3   Drink enough water to make your urine clear and you'll think more clearly too! 1.5 litres a day for the next four weeks and you will see and feel a 60 per cent improvement in your general vitality levels.

4 Tell the truth to everyone you talk to for seven days. Truth can be a great energizer.

5 Become a sleep slut – learn how to nap like an expert – gratuitously and generously.

6 Spend 10 minutes a day to lie on your bed and relax every muscle in your body.

7 Identify what person, project(s) are bleeding you dry of energy – ask yourself: 'What would I have to change about my thinking to never have another project/person bleed me dry?' What would I have to change to about my thinking to stop rescuing/stop people-pleasing/stop trying to prove that I'm good enough?

8 Say no.

9 Ask for help.

10 Ask yourself what shift you will have to make to actually be able to say 'no' or ask for help (see above list)?

Afterword

'And they lived happily ever after . . .'

Congratulations, you've just graduated from Wizard School. You've done battle with your demons, met your Inner Pessimist, recognized your scams and seen your Saboteurs – and you're still standing, wand in hand with your big wizard graduation hat on.

You're living magically, you're doing it – it is possible. People now start to take notice. You're no longer 'mad', you're 'inspirational'. People want to interview you, people want to know you, people want to be like you. You're 'there' – now what?

Many Big Leapers comment that they wish that the sun could go down and the credits would roll at this particular high moment in their journey and so they can live 'happily ever after', that they could capture that moment in time and simply hear the applause as they ride off into the sunset.

In real life, the sun comes up the next morning when we're hung-over and saddle sore, and life goes on: the kids still need feeding, the food shopping needs to be done, the car needs filling with petrol. Just because we believe in magic doesn't mean that we don't have to do the washing up.

The Inner Pessimist doesn't pack his bags either. He kicks around inside your head, knowing that it's only a matter of time before you'll have a vulnerable moment of tiredness when he can start piping up loud and strong again: 'When are you going to stop this nonsense?'

This book has been about aligning our working life with our true passions and creating an environment of enjoyment for our everyday life. And yes, it has been changing the way we 'do' things. However, the real journey is the work we have done in our heads and our hearts – and it's ongoing. To work and live in a way that delights us, we must become delighted by our world moment by moment, day by day, week by week.

In these last few pages of the book, I'm asking you to re-commit. Not to me but to yourself. To live a life based on acceptance, joy and growth instead of struggle, pain and fear. To live a magical, wizard existence, we have to make a commitment to a life listening to the voice of our Inner Coach. Not just once after reading this book but every day. It's so easy to forget who we are, how powerful we are, what we can create with our beliefs and our intentions. And we need to remind ourselves – every day.

When I first committed to finding another way, I practically glowed in the dark with happiness. 'I don't have to live like this any more', I thought. 'I don't have to do this any more. I don't have to drink to drown my sorrows, to smoke so many cigarettes it makes me retch, to fall asleep on trains miles from home.' I was a woman transformed. On the day I made that commitment, I went to bed feeling so high I couldn't sleep. The world was my oyster, no more suffering, no more stress. My life began right then.

I woke up in the morning feeling terrible. I felt thick-headed and hung-over with a tongue that didn't quite fit in my mouth. Who was I kidding? The night before, I'd planned to jump out of bed and go running. This was the new me – the new, glowing, energetic me. Instead I staggered out of bed at 10.30 after pressing the snooze button at least 20 times. I felt about as enthusiastic as Homer Simpson having to go to work on a bank holiday. But I couldn't help but smile at myself. I was like someone who decides they're going to lose weight, eats a salad for supper and then expects to wake up 3 stones lighter.

I am going to live a life of joy, delight and rapture, I intoned. I was not going to sit and sweat at my desk, I was going to go out into the world and have some fun. I was not going to suffer anymore. I was going to find another way to make my work and life a joyous experience. I was no longer going to drag myself to my desk every morning, every word written like pulling teeth. There has to be another way, there has to another way. I got out of the tube station and it started to rain, my umbrella blew inside out, I headed for my favourite café in a bookshop and arrived to find it closed. I gritted my teeth. 'There has to be another way, there has to be another way.'

The first day of my new life was spent in the most unaesthetic greasy spoon café in London with a picture of Elvis above me trying while I tried to create a vision of what I wanted my new life to look like and a plan of action of how to get there.

I was committed to finding another way to live my life. I could have stayed at home and been dry, out of the rain, without Elvis and been all smug and victim-like: 'See. This doesn't work. I knew it! Life is all about suffering.' Sigh. And to be honest, it definitely felt the most comfortable option that morning. How much easier to stay in bed and whinge about life but not do or think anything different? Unless I was truly committed, that's exactly what I would have chosen to do.

So the early days, are where you do all the hard work, it's where you take a Big Leap of faith and just trust that you have to do something different for your life to be different. Sometimes it's not even the early days. Even now I find myself sweating and toiling over a project until I remember that I simply don't suffer any more. Sometimes it's just a matter of remembering. Remembering the commitment you made to yourself and your inner coach.

Ten ways to know you're living in the world of the Inner Coach

1 You are very gentle with yourself.
2 You trust that even if something is happening right now that isn't so great, it's all happening for a reason.
3 You are learning from life's experiences.
4 You laugh – a lot more.
5 You stop taking yourself so seriously.
6 You can let go of the outcome.
7 You are kind to yourself and others.
8 You notice your inner dialogue but don't get 'caught' so often.
9 You accept yourself exactly as you are right now.
10 You meditate every day.

In the beginning, you thought in a certain way – the way you'd though all your life – so to start thinking differently and then doing things differently may just feel impossible. And with five deadlines to finish by the end of the week, with five children to get in the bath and in bed by eight, five manuscripts to read by tomorrow, £500 to find and pay by Monday – how can you possibly find another way, an easier way, an effortless way? A way that makes you smile and feel warm inside rather than so frazzled you chew the ends of your fingers down to the stumps?

It's going to take commitment. A commitment to experiment, a commitment to be curious and try a different route, even though it may feel clumsy and rather odd, a commitment to stepping out of your comfort zone, a commitment to tuning in to your Inner Coach, a commitment to meditating, a commitment to taking action based on your instincts, a commitment to trust in a magical world of 'whispers' when all logic tells you no, a commitment to thinking differently. Remember that the real Big Leap is a shift in thinking that will change your world forever. It's magical thinking. It's wizard thinking. You're one thought away from that.

A Big Leap is a radical shift in thinking, which challenges one or more of the assumptions you have previously made about life.

I'm asking you to commit to continuing to make these leaps in these very last pages because it's an on-going journey. I know what it's like to read yet another self-help book and a week later to have forgotten what it said. Even though the leap in your head can happen in an instant, you have a lifetime of old beliefs, and thought-patterns to manoeuvre around. This Big Leap journey is a commitment to the long-term. It's quite easy really. You just have to notice when you're tired, stressed or unhappy and use each miserable moment as another wake-up call. Life doesn't have to be like this. Choose another way to think. Make the leap. Once you have made that commitment you've opened the door to another life, to world of magic, and when no one is looking, you get to wear your wizard hat. Enjoy.

Further Information

CONTACT SUZY GREAVES

- For further details about workshops, talks, corporate training, products and one to one and group coaching offered by The Big Leap Coaching Company, log on to www.thebig-leap.com
- For a free half-hour trial coaching session with a Big Leap Coach, email trial@thebig-leap.com
- To receive your free Big Leap newsletter log on to www.thebig-leap.com

FURTHER READING

I have found many books useful and inspiring on the way to making my own big leap. here are a few that I particularly recommend.

Be Here Now, Ram Dass (Crown)
Powerful Beyond Measure, Nick Williams (Bantam)
The Work We Were Born to Do, Nick Williams (Element)
Finding Your Own North Star, Martha Beck (Piatkus)
A Return to Love, Marianne Williamson (Harper Collins)
A Gradual Awakening, Stephen Levine (Gateway Books)
The Portable Coach, Thomas J. Leonard (Simon Schuster)
Coach Yourself to Success, Talane Miedaner (Contemporary Books)
Feel The Fear and Do It Anyway, Susan Jeffers (Rider)
Fearless Living, Rhonda Britten (Hodder & Stoughton)
Book of Yo!, Simon Woodroffe (Capstone)

Harry Potter and the Philosopher's Stone, J. K. Rowling (Bloomsbury)
The Way of The Wizard, Deepak Chopra (Rider)
The Power of Now, Eckhart Tolle (Hodder and Stoughton)
The Purpose of Your Life, Carol Adrienne (Piatkus)
The Courage To Be Rich, Suzy Orman (Random House)
Real Wealth Creation, Stella Shamon (Orion)
Writing Down The Bones, Natalie Goldberg (Shambhala)
The Art of Effortless Living, Ingrid Bacci (Bantam)
The Joy Diet, Martha Beck (Piatkus)
Sweat Your Prayers, Gabrielle Roth (Newleaf)
Secrets of a High-Heeled Healer, Ann Marie Woodhall (HarperCollins)

USEFUL WEB ADDRESSES

- To train as a coach with Coach University, log on to: www.coachu.com

- Talane Miedaner, owner and founder of Talane Coaching Company is in the process of writing a new book on fulfilling your emotional needs. To complete a needs quiz and to find out more log on to: www.lifecoach.com

- Rachel Pryor, highly qualified, coaches clients around 21st century wealth creation and careers.
  www.meunltd.com.
  01225 427771

- Join Nick Williams' inspirational dreambuilders community on: www.dreambuilderscommunity.com

- To help you further identity your needs, log on to The Enneagram Institute's website and take their free test www.enneagraminstitute.com

- For support in building your business contact Ginny Baillie at Baillie and Friends, who runs The Success Club, a four-month success programme for sole traders who want to accelerate their business and increase their professional network.
  www.thesuccessclub.org
  01873 857344.

- When you need to re-charge the batteries, book a retreat with the brilliant team at The Retreat Company.
  www.theretreatcompany.com

- When you need to feel fabulous contact Tramp2Vamp!, a personal styling service run by Big Leaper Nicky Hambleton-Jones.
  www.tramp2vamp.com

- To correct posture problems and achieve an optimal state of health and fitness the pain-free way, contact Donal Doherty.
  www.egoscue.com

- To hire Salma Shah, Life Coach and Big Leaper, log on to:
  www.lifeskills-co.com

- For more information on Transcendental Meditation:
  www.tm.org or www.t-m.org.uk

Acknowledgements

I wouldn't be here writing this book if it weren't for my first coach Rachel Pryor (www.meunltd.com), one of the most skilled and brilliant coaches in the world. She was my very first coach and it was Rachel, who introduced me to the concepts of scams and beliefs and has helped me formulate many of the ideas for this book. She has changed my life.

A huge thanks to all my wonderful Big Leapers – Nicky, Donal, Lynne, Rachel, Andrew, Chris and Salma. Your courage and magnificence has inspired me on every page. You have been a joy to coach. Thank you to all the unidentified Big Leapers too – I know who you are and take my hat off to you.

I would also like to thank all my coaches throughout my seven-year journey: Doug Scroggins, Harriet Simon Salinger, Nick Williams, Arlene Mann, Gabriella Goddard. Your inspiration and wisdom have helped me transform my life.

Big thanks to Ginny Baillie and Talene Miedaner for their help with my last minute panic when writing about needs. Talene is currently in the process of writing a whole book on how to get our needs met – go to www.lifecoach.com find out more.

This book would never have been written without the wisdom of the founder of Coach University, Thomas Leonard.

Thanks to my agent Fiona Spencer Thomas for her untiring support and loyalty.

Thanks to Jo Hemmings, Jane Morrow and the team at New Holland Publishers for your enthusiasm and belief in me. And massive thanks to Deborah Taylor, who has edited these pages so brilliantly and effortlessly.

Thanks to Martha Beck for her inspiration on the journalistic exercises. Read her book: *Finding Your Own North Star* for more inspiration on making your Big Leap.

And I wouldn't be sane if it weren't for my good friends Rachel and Caroline, who have done everything from babysit to send me Bridget Jones novels when my metaphysical ramblings started to get them worried.

Huge thanks to my husband Jools for feeding me, filling the fridge and baby-sitting for weeks while I beavered away.

And a big kiss to my own Inner Coach, who finally managed to speak up enough for this process to be as enjoyable as writing a book could be.

Index